The Architecture of MUSEUMS

Author

Francisco Asensio Cerver

Editorial manager

Paco Asensio

Project coordinator

Ivan Bercedo (Architect)

Graphic Design

Mireia Casanovas Soley

Layout

Òscar Lleonart Ruiz

Text

Ivan Bercedo: *Introduction. The Menil Collection Museum and Cy Twombly*
Annex. Natural History Museum, Rotterdam.
Stiklestad Cultural Center. San Francisco Museum of Modern Art.
Chikatsu-Asuka Historical Museum. The Guggenheim Museum. P.S.1 Museum
The Institute for Contemporary Art. The Old Provence Research Institute.
Natural History Museum, London Primates Gallery and Earth Galleries. Chiado
Museum.
Anna Puyuelo: *Domus.*
Itziar Sen: *Museum of Modern Art and Wakayama Prefectural Museum.*
Arken Museum of Modern Art. Deer Valley Rock Art Museum.
Okazaki Art and Historical Museum. Shoji Ueda Museum of Photography.
Kunsthal. Lecture Hall and West Wing of the Brooklyn Museum.

Translation

Mark Lodge

Copyediting

Michael Webb

Proofreading

Amber Ockrassa

First published in 1997 by Arco for

Hearst Books International

1350 Avenue of the Americas

New York, NY 10019

Distributed in the U.S. and Canada by

Watson-Guptill Publications

1515 Broadway

New York, NY 10036

Distributed throughout the rest of the world by

Hearst Books international

1350 Avenue of the Americas

New York, NY 10019

1997 © Francisco Asensio Cerver

ISBN: 0-8230-6131-0

Printed in Spain

The Architecture of Museums

Introduction **6**

Deer Valley Rock Art Museum. William P. Bruder **8**

San Francisco Museum of Modern Art. Mario Botta **20**

The Menil Collection Museum and Cy Twombly Annex. Renzo Piano **32**

P.S.1 Museum, The Institute for Contemporary Art. Frederick Fisher **42**

Lecture Hall and West Wing of the Brooklyn Museum. Arata Isozaki / James Stewart Polshek **50**

Domus. Arata Isozaki y César Portela **60**

The Guggenheim Museum. Frank O. Gehry **72**

Arken Museum of Modern Art. Soren Robert Lund **84**

Natural History Museum, Rotterdam. Erik van Egeraat **96**

The Old Provence Research Institute. Henri E. Ciriani **108**

Kunsthal. Rem Koolhaas **120**

Natural History Museum, London Primates Gallery and Earth Galleries. Terry Pawson / Keith Williams **128**

Chiado Museum. Jean Michel Paul Wilmotte **136**

Stiklestad Cultural Center. Jens Petter Askim **144**

Okazaki Art and Historical Museum. Akira Kuryu **154**

Shoji Ueda Museum of Photography. Shin Takamatsu **162**

Chikatsu-Asuka Historical Museum. Tadao Ando **172**

Museum of Modern Art and Wakayama Prefectural Museum. Kisho Kurokawa **178**

Biographies **190**

If there is one building that symbolizes modern thinking, it is the museum. The roots of both private collections and large public museums go back no further than the past century. The interest in compiling in an orderly and systematic fashion objects and works of arts from all ages is an essentially modern phenomenon. No previous civilization had looked to the past in such a structured, analytical manner. The museum came into existence at the same time as scientific thinking became consolidated and the first systematic treatises on history were published.

However, contrary to appearance, the need to discover the past and have convenient access to it in public galleries reveals, paradoxically, a break between the present and the immediate past. When the culture of a people that lived two thousand years ago or on the other side of the world becomes a presence equivalent to that of our grandparents, it means that the passing on of knowledge does not occur linearly. In this sense, the museum is a building that reveals and symbolizes modern thinking.

The technological revolution arising from the development of information technology and the media has undoubtedly led to a transformation of museums. It is not that what is past is out of date; what will happen within two years time is already out of date. Virtual reality enables us to witness fashions long before they reach the market. Magazines and the specialized press provide designers with projects in the making, and when they are actually realized, the underlying ideas have already been discussed, altered, debated, and even surpassed.

Novelty is so ephemeral and cycles so short that they cease to exist. Logic has accelerated to such an extent that it becomes simultaneous and perpetual. Museums of all kinds are being opened: local museums, museums of wine, shoes, coffee, or Dada. At the same time, traditional museums are oversized, making it impossible to visit them in a single day. They move beyond their traditional function and take on others. They are equipped for people

wishing to relax, shop, or have a meal. They organize seminars and postgraduate courses. As the monuments that identify and differentiate cities, they are turned into tourist attractions, act as art markets, promote certain artists to the detriment of others, and anticipate fashions by organizing temporary exhibitions.

Museums can be visited not only in person but also via Internet or television documentaries. Thus, the process of acceleration has not only failed to close museums, but rather has served to further validate their existence. Like stories by Borges and Calvino in which metaphor and reality finally merge, museums have changed from being a reflection of culture to being symmetrical to it.

Despite the efforts of exhibition and museum directors, presenting a work of art in a museum involves, in most cases, taking it out of context. Until recently, the only way a resident of London could discover Egyptian culture was through history books and the British Museum. Today, the widespread phenomenon of tourism makes it as likely that the Londoner will visit Luxor itself as the British Museum. For that reason, the museum should seek to become an extension of a piece, a form of explaining and enriching it.

To place a work by Ryman next to one by Schnabel, or a Turrell next to a Häring with a card underneath that reads "Untitled, 1993/mixed techniques," can lead to confusion. It is enormously difficult to understand the significance of an author's work separate from the rest, because they generally form a series; and the work is even more difficult to understand when it is placed next to those of other artists whose ideas are totally different.

Museums can, and should, be buildings designed to offer information and broaden our knowledge of a subject. They can also, however, become pure, senseless confusion in which all the works are taken out of context and converted into mere images -inert and unintelligent. The work of museum directors and architects is to prevent that.

The Architecture of Museums

Deer Valley Rock Art Museum

William P. Bruder

Architecture must take into account the characteristics of the chosen site –the mountains, water, arid land, heat– and it must capture how nature changes throughout the day and the seasons. It must remind us of the landscape and expose its scars. Only in this way can architecture create an inhabitable, meaningful space for the present and the past.

A large part of the present American landscape can no longer be seen as a series of well-defined individual spaces such as farms, ranches and fields, but rather as areas established and bounded by roads and freeways. It is no longer architecture that provides the relevant landmarks. The Arizona desert, however, is one of the few spaces where architecture maintains its artistic and symbolic functions. It is here where William Bruder has been developing his work since the end of the 'seventies.

Taking up once more subjects raised by Wright, his architecture reveals how he occupies the landscape using highly elaborate geometric forms and local materials that obscure the limits of his architecture, integrating the project into the desert. This initially hostile environment is transformed, softened, and finally integrated into the architecture.

Location: *Deer Valley, Phoenix, Arizona, USA.*
Design date: *1995.*
Architect: *William P. Bruder.*
Collaborators: *Wendell Burnette, Bob Adams, Beau Dromiack, Rick Joy, Maryann Bloomfield.*
Photography: *Bill Timmerman.*

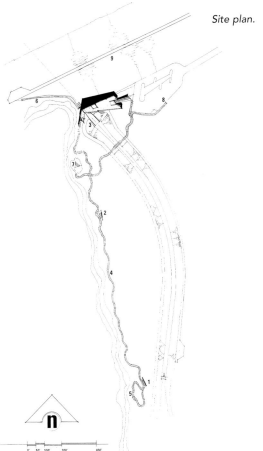

Site plan.

In the same way that architecture influences the landscape by creating new landmarks, the surroundings also alter the architecture. The wind and rain will leave a layer of rust on the steel, the light will gradually alter the colors, and extreme temperatures will etch broken lines on the facings. "This is like a constructed ruin," explains Bruder. "Although I wonder about our fascination with ruins, I also think they get us beyond temporal and surface considerations, down to the bare root."

Bruder's architectural training was somewhat unconventional. He combined his academic studies at the University of Wisconsin School of Sculpture with his practical work as a builder at Wenzler's studio. He met and worked with Bruce Goff until, in 1974, he obtained his architect's degree and opened his own office. A decisive moment in Bruder's career was his stay at the American Academy in Rome in 1987. There he discovered the work of Carlo Scarpa, the spatial quality of his architecture, his concern for detail and materials, textures, and weights. This signals a before and after in Bruder's work and, as he himself states, his projects became more stylized, more illuminated, a combination of the most essential elements as an expression of minimalization.

The dark sand becomes a wall, the light is filtered through perforated plates and slots, the shadows harden, the paved floor stretches out to welcome the tired visitor.

The Deer Valley Rock Art Center near Phoenix, Arizona, was built in 1994 over a water course. The building has been designed as a funnel that channels the visitors from the parking lot toward the mountain and the petroglyphs engraved by the Hohokam Indians. The ground floor is a triangle framed by the mountain and a dike, linking together civilization and nature. The building becomes a time tunnel, a door to hidden knowledge, a path to the works of art. This is the symbolic value of the museum. The emotions unleashed by the architecture prepare the way for the contemplation of the works, because Bruder's intention is that the building itself act as a text.

Bruder has organized the floor longitudinally to create two parallel itineraries: a continuous one that houses the museum, and another, more private, itinerary that houses the reception area, archive, offices, and classrooms. The structure of beams and metal pillars, parallel to this line, rises above the facings to create a continuous perspective reminiscent of an industrial bay. The roof slopes on both sides.

Bruder chooses his materials with a purpose: he wants the building to be visually integrated into the landscape, to appear as another geographical feature, a line, a scar, and so he employs prefabricated concrete slabs clad in an aggregate taken from the dark rock of the Arizona desert mountains.

General plan.

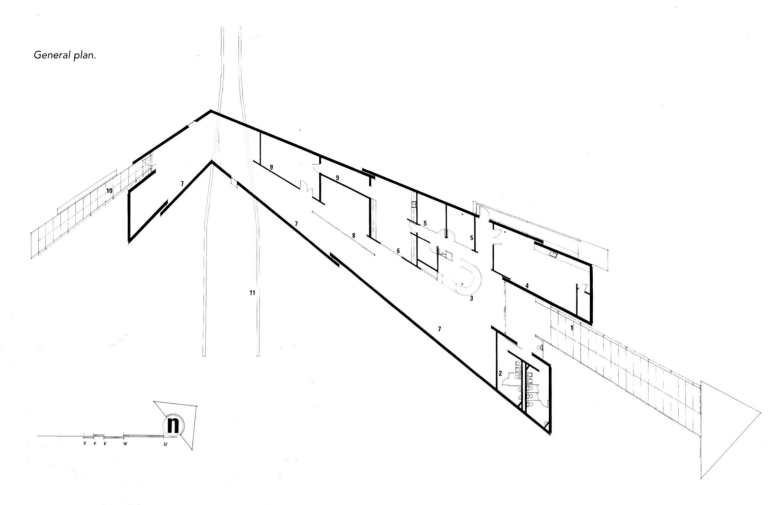

In the longitudinal section, the highest point coincides with the water course and marks a turning point. Transversely, the roof opens up toward the exhibition area, increasing the amount of free space. There is a single level which is entered via a gentle ramp from the parking lot. Cor-Ten metal plates welcome the visitor, creating a shaded path that leads toward the reception area and acts as a transition between the blinding desert light and the filtered illumination inside the Rock Art Center. Bruder has chosen to create an opaque box with incisions that illuminate specific points or sequences, while the strategically placed windows enable the visitor to look out at the rocks. The Center also offers a vantage point over the dike and the landscape.

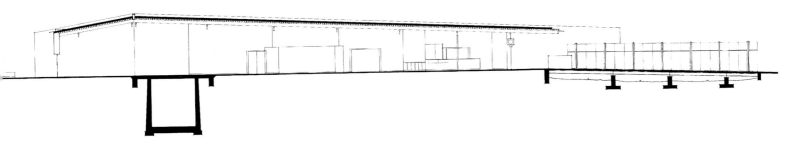

Section.

San Francisco Museum of Modern Art

Mario Botta

In today's city, the museum plays a role analogous to that of the cathedral of yesterday, a place we require in order to challenge the hopes and contradictions of our times. It is also a place where the values and aesthetics of the past are very much present and which bear witness to the unique sensibilities of mankind throughout history. In fact, it might be possible to interpret the museum as a space dedicated to witnessing and searching for a new religiosity, which promotes and enriches those spiritual values that we so strongly need. (Mario Botta)

The central theme in Mario Botta's work is the restoration of monumentality.

His projects reflect a quality often lacking in modern architecture but which has been associated with this art for centuries. Botta uses many of the architectural features common to this type of building' simple, hermetic volumes, and large masses clad in brick or stone that reveal nothing about their interior. Lighting is provided by narrow slights and openings in the walls, neither readily recognizable as "windows."

Botta often organizes his projects in symmetrical fashion, both the plan and the external image of the building. The SFMOMA is structured along well-defined axes, in the Beaux-Arts tradition.

Location: *San Francisco, California, USA.*
Design date: *1991.*
Completion date: *1995.*
Architect: *Mario Botta.*
Collaborators: *Hellmuth, Obata & Kassabaum, Bechtel International Company.*
Photography: *Robert Canfield.*

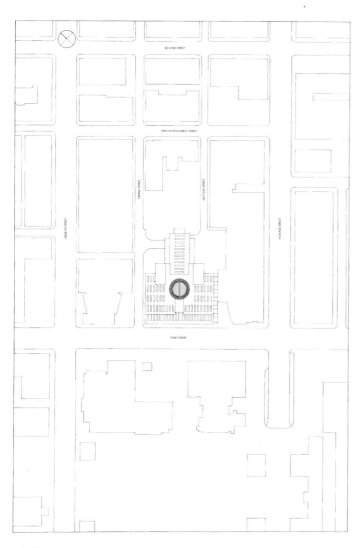

The SFMOMA forms part of a series of cultural centers recently built in San Francisco city center by internationally renowned architects. Facing the Museum, on the opposite side of Third Street, are the Yerba Buena Gardens which contain the Visual Arts Center, designed by Fumihiko Maki and the Center for the Theater Arts, by James Stewart Polshek, both inaugurated in 1994. A park has also opened recently near the museum; it was designed by Romaldo Giurgola and contains the Martin Luther King, Jr., Memorial by the artist Houstin Conwill.

Main façade.

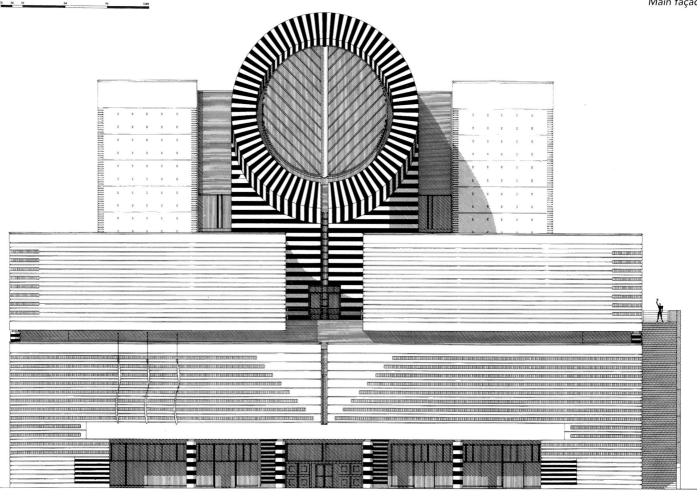

Preliminary sketches.

For over half a century, the War Veterans Memorial Building was the seat of the SFMOMA. On the occasion of the fiftieth anniversary of its foundation in 1935, its directors decided on the construction of a new building. The project, designed by the Swiss architect Mario Botta and led by the Hellmuth, Obata & Kassabaum office in San Francisco, was developed through several phases during the early 'nineties until 1995 saw its definitive completion in time for its sixtieth anniversary.

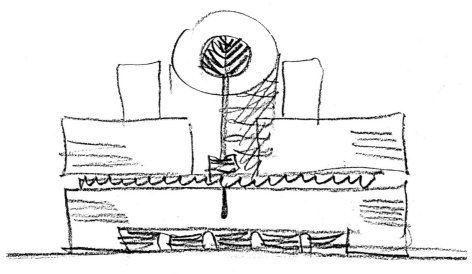

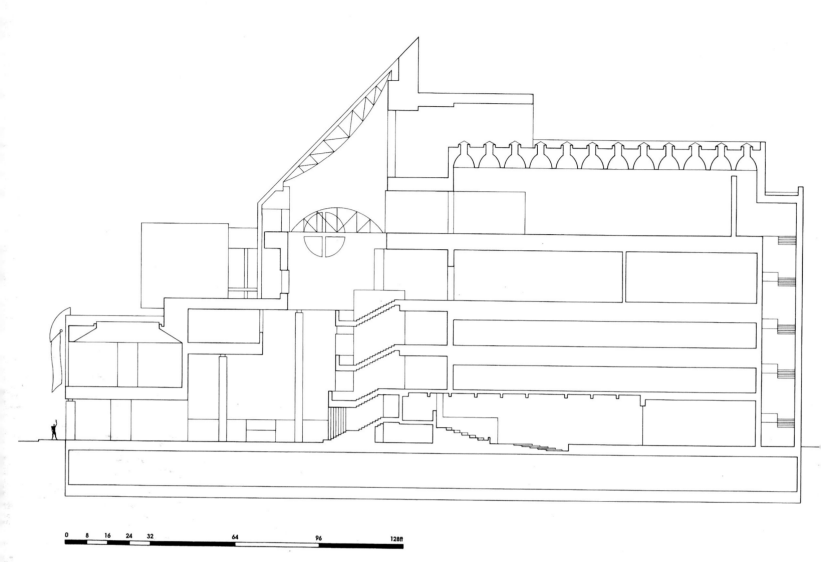

0   8   16   24   32   64   96   128ft

Botta has clearly defined a main façade, a rear façade and two side façades, the main one being the most elaborate. The building is not only perfectly symmetrical but it conforms to a volumetric hierarchy, with the highest point in the center, then falling away toward the sides. It is hardly surprising, therefore, that the San Francisco Museum of Modern Art should be so reminiscent of an ancient temple, a Mayan pyramid, or perhaps a Mesopotamian ziggurat.

Unlike most modern museums, the vast majority of which are built on the outskirts of cities, the SFMOMA is situated in a city center. The visitors' entrance is on Third Street. Two apartment blocks are planned on either side of the

museum and, at the rear, the Pacific Telephone skyscraper, completed in the 1920s.

Botta has explained that the densely built-up surroundings led him to design a large atrium, a form of covered central square inside the museum. This decision solved one of the major problems the architect has identified in today's museums: the visitor has no clear idea of the layout of the exhibition rooms. That is not the case for the SFMOMA. The central atrium interconnects all the rooms, enabling visitors to orient themselves and choose the rooms they wish to visit.

The lot for the museum has an area of 5,575 square meters (60,000 square feet), while the total built-up surface is

The outer walls are uncovered brick, except for the cylindrical tower that covers the central atrium, which is clad in black and white stone. The large skylight of the atrium is one of the most outstanding features of the overall composition.

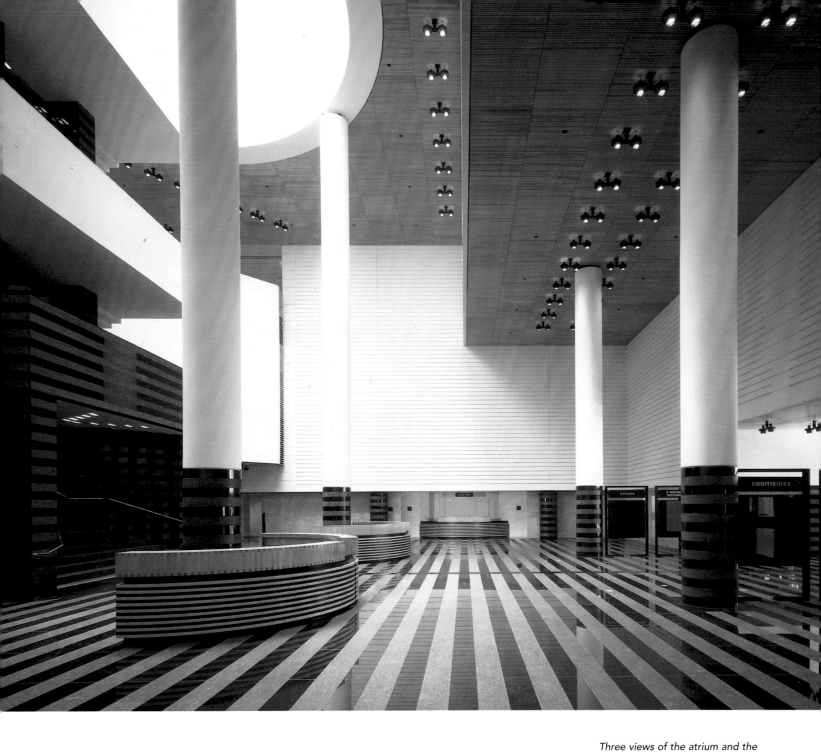

Three views of the atrium and the main staircase. The interior maintains the same symmetry as the façade. The hall is of a monumental character, as is the entire building. Botta uses the contrast of dark and light bands for the floor surface, the stairs, and the counters.

The staircase, however, is ceremonial in style. Ascending it to the exhibition rooms becomes virtually a ritual.

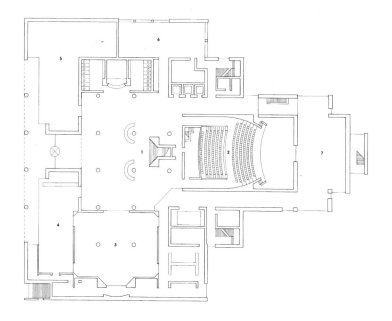

Ground floor.

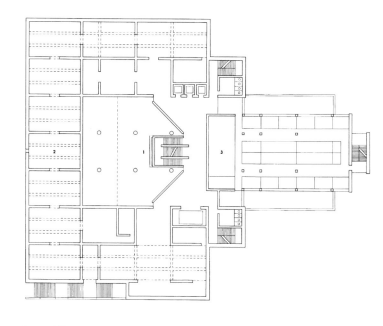

Second floor.

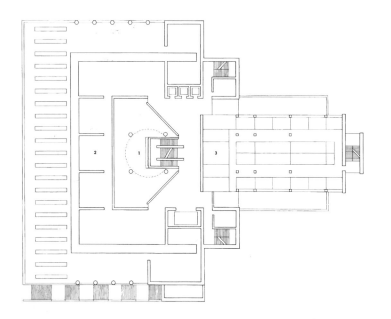

Third floor.

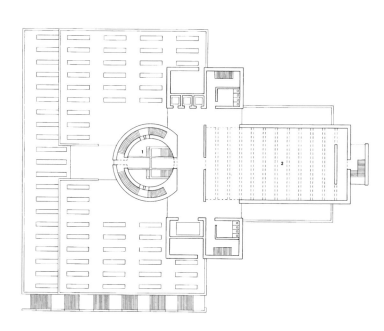

Fourth floor.

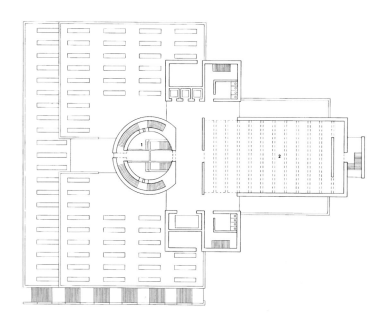

Fifth floor

The architects to whom Mario Botta refers as his "masters" are Louis I. Kahn, Le Courbusier (with whom he worked on the Venice hospital project), and Carlo Scarpa (examiner of his graduation paper). His work, nevertheless, reflects a strong classical influence and influence of the Beaux-Arts tradition.

20,500 square meters (220,000 square feet). In addition to the exhibition rooms, it comprises a 200-seat auditorium, multiple-use event spaces, library, book-store, workshops, conservation areas (the SFMOMA department is internationally recognized for its conservation of 20th century art), offices, and a cafeteria.

Although the building has six floors, Botta has achieved one of his original aims: to illuminate most of the rooms with natural top lighting. This was made possible by using a "staggered" design. On the ground floor are all the independent areas, such as the book-shop, cafeteria, temporary exhibition area, and main hall. The exhibition rooms are situated on the upper floors. Botta uses this staggered structure, from the main façade back to the rear, to situate the rooms only at the sides that have no upper floor, leaving the rest for offices or conservation rooms. Thus, the exhibition areas form a stair-case and the lower volumes are taken up with the remaining facilities.

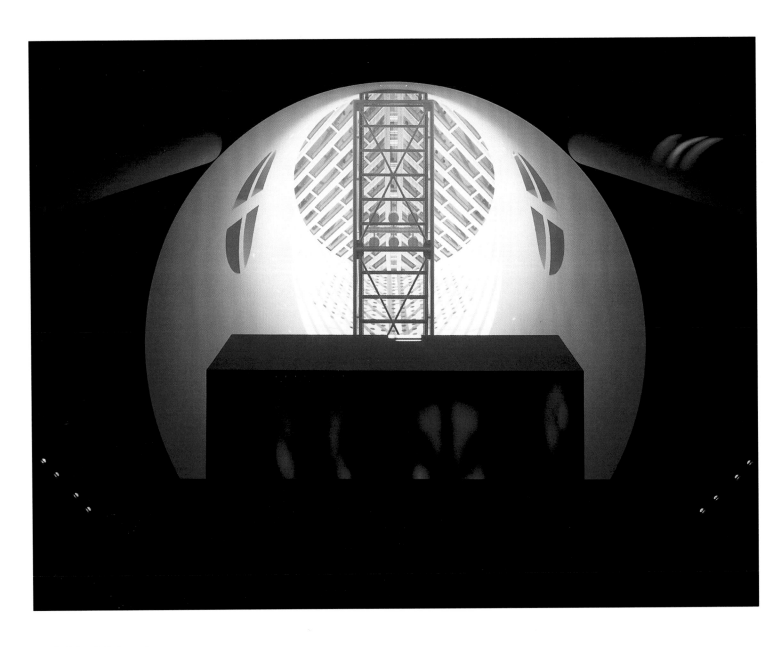

Detail of the skylight and
cross section.

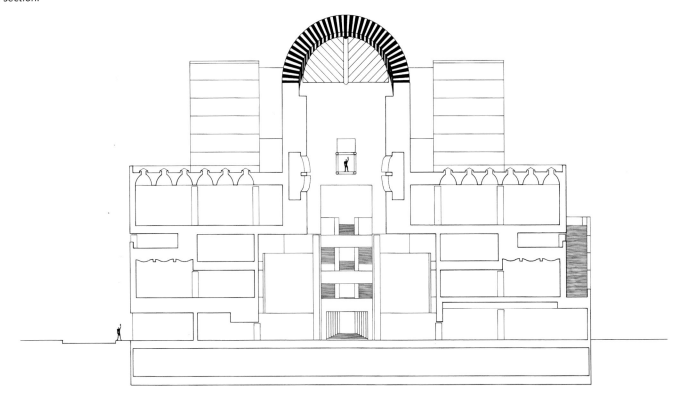

Construction detail and perspective, in which the natural lighting of the rooms can be seen.

View of one of the exhibition rooms.

De Menil Collection Museum and Cy Twombly Annex

Renzo Piano

In 1981, Dominique de Menil commissioned Renzo Piano, co-designer of the Pompidou Center in Paris, together with Richard Rogers, with the design of the new building for her collection of surrealistic and primitive African art. The site for the museum was a residential area in Houston, Texas, comprising small bungalows built in the 19th century. Piano designed a museum to human scale, a building with no monumental pretensions, which fits perfectly into this setting. Both the scale and the choice of finish are adapted to the context and local tradition, yet without relinquishing the use of sophisticated construction elements.

In a certain sense, this museum is the antithesis of the Pompidou Center. Indeed, in the projects developed by Piano subsequent to the Pompidou Center, technology is used to make full use of light, context, and integration into nature. If the Pompidou Center has an industrial appearance, the rest of Piano's work reveals an ecological motivation. Technology has ceased to be a method and an end in itself; it is now only a method.

Technology was applied in the Pompidou Center to regenerate a decaying area which the Paris Council sought to revitalize with the construction of a major

Location: *Houston, Texas, USA.*

De Menil Collection
Design date: *1981.*
Completion date: *1986.*
Collaborators: *S. Ishida, M. Carroll, M. Downs, C. Patel, B. Plattner, C. Susstrunk.*

Cy Twombly Annex
Design date: *1992.*
Completion date: *1995.*
Collaborators: *S. Ishida, M. Carroll, M. Palmore.*

Photography: *Hickey + Robertson.*

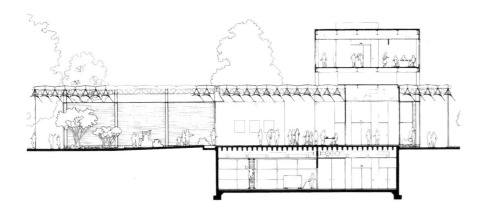

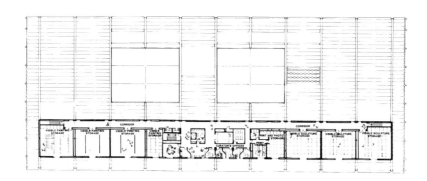

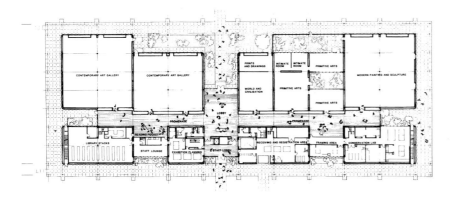

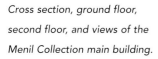

Cross section, ground floor,
second floor, and views of the
Menil Collection main building.

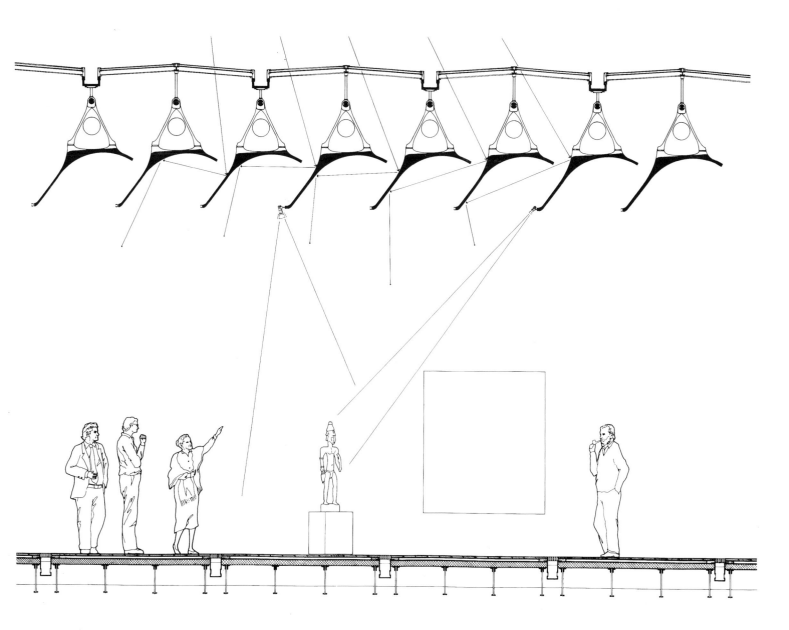

Detail of the roof.

This roof, designed by Renzo Piano's office, together with the prestigious engineering office of Ove Arup, adapts to the angles of incidence of the sun's rays, creates multiple refractions, and filters the ultraviolet rays to form a "solar machine." All necessary conditioning facilities are located under the wooden floor.

cultural and tourist complex. Dominique de Menil's aim was exactly the opposite; her museum was to share not only the atmosphere of its surroundings, but also to become a kind of cultural village. The Cy Twombly Annex, situated on the far side of one of the streets surrounding the main building, together with the location of several museum sections in neighboring bungalows, completes the transformation of a residential village into a cultural one.

It is common to use existing buildings as museums, yet this is not the case of the De Menil Collection. Here, only the most familiar features of the context have been used. The museum itself is a new building, specif-

ically planned to provide the most suitable itineraries, room size and lighting for the visitors to appreciate the works on display.

Another aim has been to design a roof that would admit natural light, prevent reflections, and allow the intensity of the light to be adjusted to reflect changes in time and season. This was achieved by use of a series of filters and several enormous, prefabricated concrete "leaves" which constitute the main element of the project.

The number of works on display is deliberately limited to no more than two or three hundred, which are in constant rotation. This allows the visitor to enjoy certain pieces while enabling the museum's team

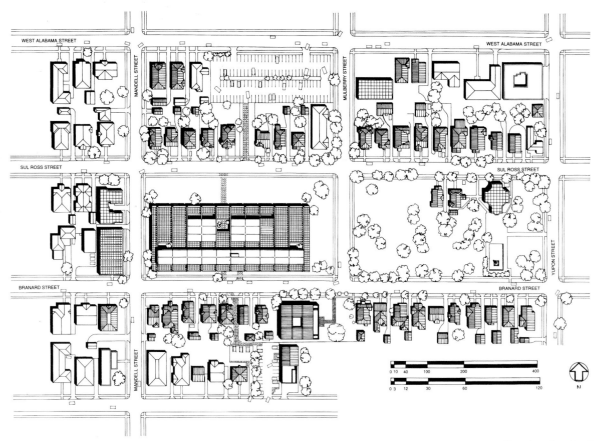

Site plan showing buildings and the
neighboring bungalows.

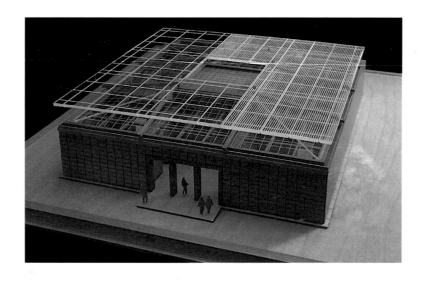

Elevations.

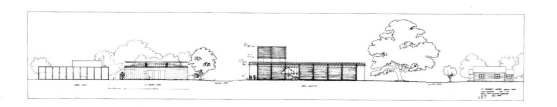

of curators to maintain the works regularly. Five years after the main building was opened, Dominique de Menil commissioned Renzo Piano with the design of a small exhibition space measuring approximately 835 square meters (9,000 square feet) as an annex to the museum, devoted to the works of the American abstract-expressionist artist Cy Twombly.

The appearance of this building is different from that of the main building, on the express wishes of both the owner and the architect. Nevertheless, they share the same concern: lighting. Working together with Ove Arup, the Department of Architecture and Urban Planning at the University of Michigan carried out lighting studies. A model of the building was placed under a large, spherical mirror and by means of a complex system of computer-controlled lamps the movement and

intensity of the Houston sun was reproduced in order to study its effects on the building's interior. The purpose of these studies was to assess the possibility of having a roof formed by a series of successive filters that would reduce the light's intensity to suitable levels, yet without concealing its ever-changing nature.

Exterior views. The annex is on the same scale as the bungalows that surround it. Unlike the façades of the main building, the façades of the annex deliberately contrast with those of the neighboring bungalows.

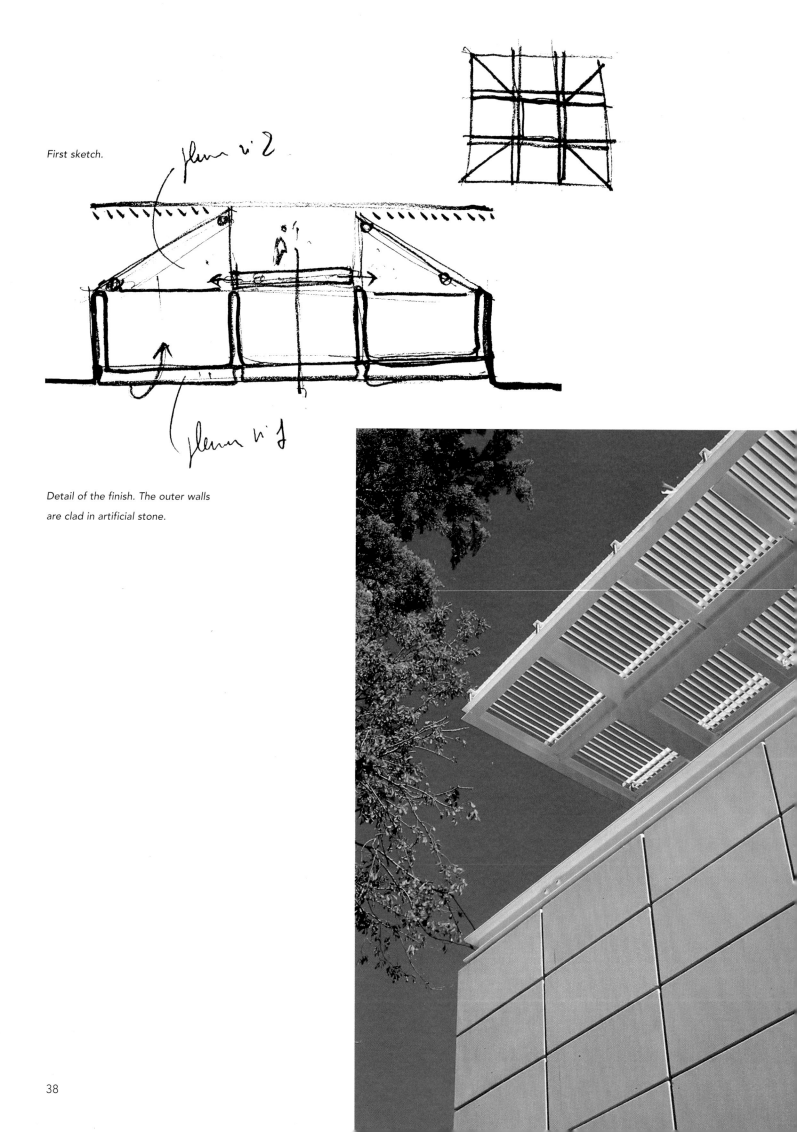

First sketch.

*Detail of the finish. The outer walls
are clad in artificial stone.*

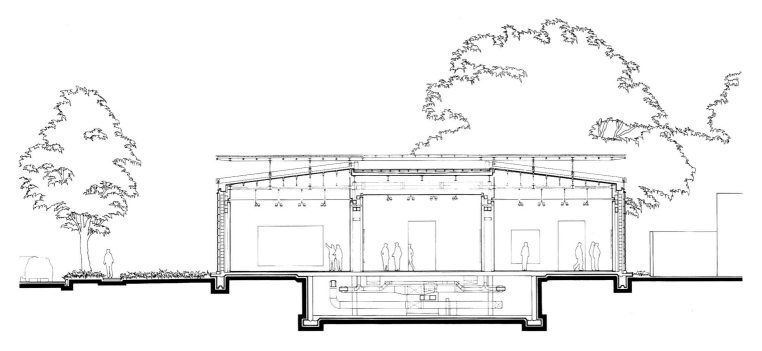

Construction section.

Ground floor.

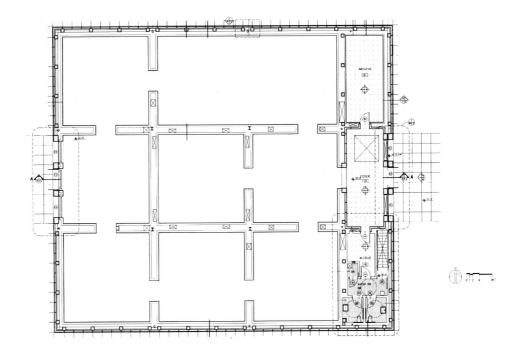

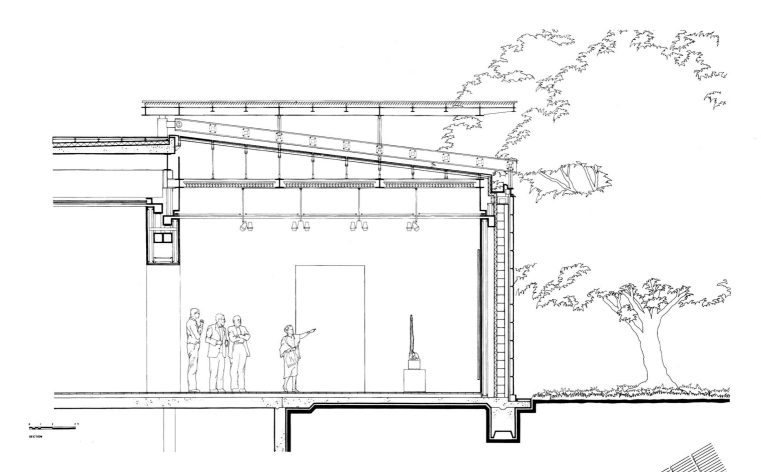

SECTION

Details of the roof. The definitive roof comprises five different layers: a first layer of fixed leaves, a white, grid-like, steel structure; an adjustable glass louvre to block out ultraviolet rays; another, movable louvre; and the last layer, which forms the ceiling of the exhibition rooms, consisting of semi-transparent fabric. This fabric, in Piano's own words, represents a blank canvas ready for the artist to start working on.

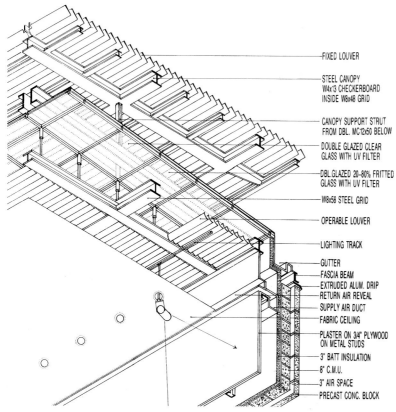

- FIXED LOUVER
- STEEL CANOPY W4x13 CHECKERBOARD INSIDE W8x48 GRID
- CANOPY SUPPORT STRUT FROM DBL. MC12x50 BELOW
- DOUBLE GLAZED CLEAR GLASS WITH UV FILTER
- DBL.GLAZED 20-80% FRITTED GLASS WITH UV FILTER
- W8x58 STEEL GRID
- OPERABLE LOUVER
- LIGHTING TRACK
- GUTTER
- FASCIA BEAM
- EXTRUDED ALUM. DRIP
- RETURN AIR REVEAL
- SUPPLY AIR DUCT
- FABRIC CEILING
- PLASTER ON 3/4" PLYWOOD ON METAL STUDS
- 3" BATT INSULATION
- 6" C.M.U.
- 3" AIR SPACE
- PRECAST CONC. BLOCK

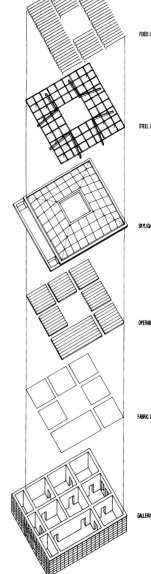

FIXED LOUV

STEEL CAN

SKYLIGHT

OPERABLE

FABRIC CEIL.

GALLERIES

As if to counterbalance the complexity of the roof, the floor layout is extremely simple: the exhibition area is a perfect square, divided into nine equal squares, one for each room.

Unlike the transparent roof, the perimetral walls admit virtually no light, except for the entrance and its opposite in the rear façade. The lack of windows frees the entire wall space for hanging paintings while avoiding distracting reflections.

Several interior views. To a visitor walking around the rooms of the Cy Twombly Annex, it seems as though the fine fabric hanging on the walls conceals the sky, as if the roof of the museum were the canopy of a house next to the sea. A passing cloud darkens the room for an instant. An architect may make use of striking shapes to surprise the visitor; Piano has chosen other methods.

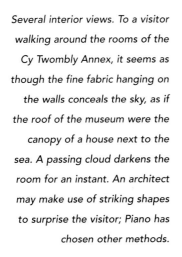

P.S.1 Museum, The Institute for Contemporary Art

Frederick Fisher

The P.S.1 Museum of the Institute for Contemporary Art, in Long Island. New York, is the result of a metamorphosis. Known as P.S.1 in the 1970s, this avant-garde art space played a leading role in the movement to take art out of traditional museums and put it into the streets and communities. Under the sensitive but firm guidance of Californian architect Frederick Fisher, P.S.1 has come of age, growing into a dynamic, multi-spaced and multi-faceted complex without losing touch with its original spirit.

With his background in art and his reputation for innovative design of museums, galleries, and artists' studios since his firm was established in 1980, Frederick Fisher was clearly an appropriate choice to undertake this scheme. He is known to respect and place great importance on the art to be housed in his spaces. Characteristically, he worked for six months developing the project's program, in close conjunction with the cultural and administrative organizations responsible. As Joseph Giovannini has

Location: *Long Island, New York, USA.*
Completion date: *1997.*
Architect: *Frederick Fisher, David Ross, Joseph Coriaty.*
Photography: *Michael Moran.*

*A new main entrance to P.S.1.,
which visitors approach
through a dramatic series of
new outdoor installation
spaces, utilizes P.S.1.' s unique
site to full advantage.*

*View of an exterior space designed
by Frederick Fisher.*

Axonometry.

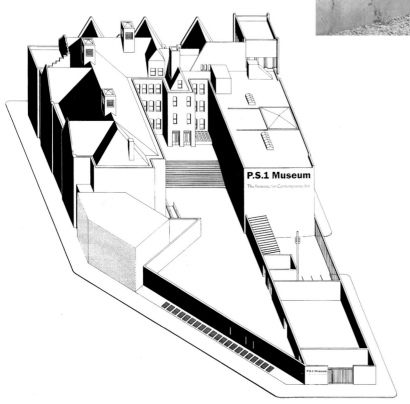

P.S.1 Museum
The Institute for Contemporary Art

P.S.1 Museum

said, "Fisher conceives his projects in spatial volumes' from the inside."

As a 19th century school in an industrial neighborhood, this 84,000-square-foot building has an enormous variety of indoor and outdoor spaces. The cultural program and the design were developed in unison to maximize these spaces, the natural light, and the various surfaces. The main entrance was moved to the rear, so that access is through a series of yard-like spaces. Inside the complex, a new entry terrace created storage space below; on the

The renovation and expansion of P.S.1. was developed with respect to the potential of the original structure, a 19th-century Gothic Revival School building.

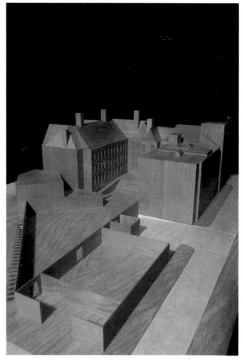

same level the reception area was expanded to include a café, bookstore, and more gallery space.

In a bid to work within the limited budget creatively, Fisher maintained and made a feature of certain emblematic elements of the original P.S.1: the central stairway, the classroom galleries, and old surfaces.

Apart from exhibition spaces, the new P.S.1 Museum has site-specific installations, an artist-in-residence and youth program, publications, technical services, and administration.

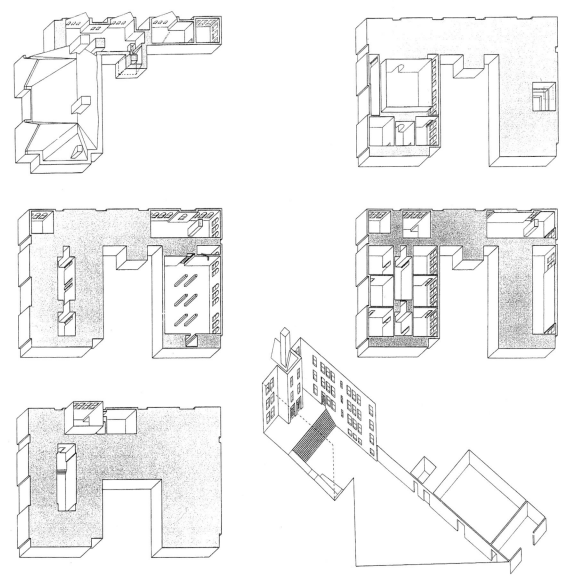

Among the new spaces are
a monumental, double-
height ceiling; a square
exhibition gallery flanked by
two long corridors with
natural light; a full-floor
gallery with windows on
both sides, two rows of
columns, and a reinforced
concrete floor, ideal for
displaying sculpture; an
intimate, brick duplex
gallery featuring an upper-
level balcony for viewing;
and a performance and
video/film theater.

Fisher has improved the structure
while maintaining its distinctive
character. By revealing the building's
underlying architectural elements, he
has provided the maximum amount
and variety of exhibition spaces.

Lecture Hall and West Wing of the Brooklyn Museum

Arata Isozaki and Associates/James Stewart Polshek and Partners

The museum, since the time of its appearance during the Enlightenment, has been the traditional institution for the public development of culture. In the same way as theaters, libraries, or the conservation of historical monuments, modern public administrations have undertaken the creation and promotion of these buildings whose existence had previously been tied exclusively to wealth and power. Social welfare is associated not only with domestic comforts or social security but also with access to a symbolical universe represented by art, travel, science, and history. From this point of view it is unsurprising that one of the aims of modern societies has been to broaden and facilitate access to cultural wealth. The Brooklyn museum project should be considered from that perspective.

When art or knowledge are no longer the exclusive property of princes and priests, but are displayed before the common people, there must exist a form of expression or language for presenting these symbols in an organized manner.

Location: *Brooklyn, New York, U.S.A.*
Architect: *Arata Isozaki/ James Stewart Polshek*
Design date: *1989.*
Completion date: *1992.*
Collaborators: *Robert Silman Associates (costruction), Goldman Copeland Batlan (mechanics), Jules Fisher & Paul Marantz (lighting), Peter George Associates (acoustics), Chapman Ducibella (security).*
Photography: *David Cardelús.*

Aspect of the main façade designed by McKim, Mead and White in 1893, of which only part was completed.

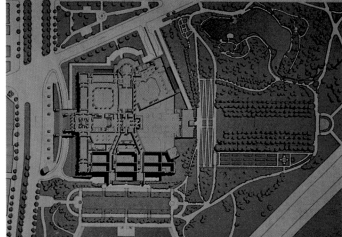

General plan.

Section.

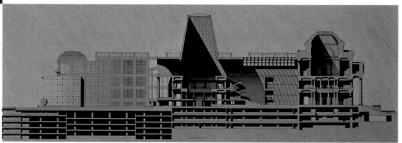

Detail of side façade.

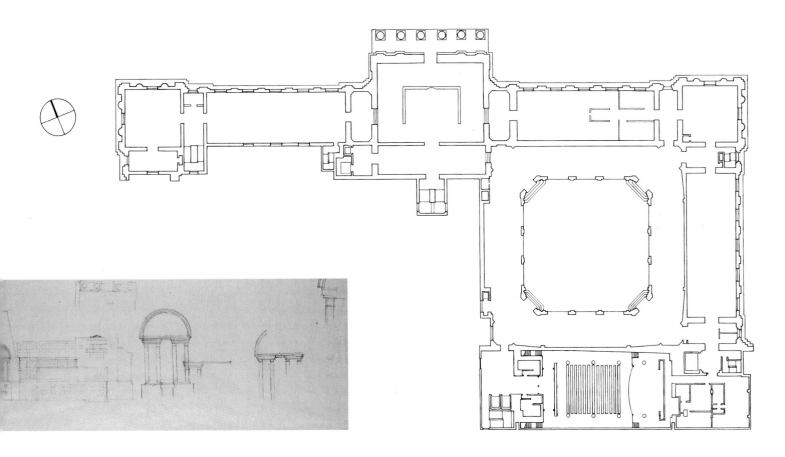

Plan of the original building and the recent enlargement performed by Arata Isozaki and James Stewart Polshek.

Thus, the architecture of the museum must efficiently explain and interpret the contents for the public. Buildings designed exclusively as museums are a relatively recent phenomenon. The museum as a public place, intended for accumulating knowledge in the form of a collection of objects, has existed only since the Enlightenment.

The construction of the Brooklyn museum was based on the design proposed by McKim, Mead and White, the winners of the competition in 1893. The original project consisted of a central obelisk surrounded by several courtyards in perfect Beaux-Arts style. Of the original plan, only the front wing and façade, along with one quadrant with a courtyard, were completed. During the more than 100 years since its construction and subsequent enlargements, the concept and requirements of the museum have changed. In 1986 a new competition was won by the project proposed by Arata Isozaki and James Stewart Polshek.

The original plan was abandoned in 1934 when the grand staircase at the entrance was demolished and other modifications were carried out. The new project includes the construction of an auditorium, provides storage space for the works, and redesigns the west wing to rationalize its use.

Views of the contemporary

art rooms.

The aim is to respect the existing approach while simultaneously reinterpreting it. The idea of the central space and independent, peripheral spaces linked to the center has been maintained. Each part has its on shape, yet all must form together a single, orderly pattern. The plan, volume, and elements are geometrically combined. Unlike the concept of rationalist architecture which favors spatial continuity, this treatment of the design creates a building made up of independent spaces. It offers a reinterpretation of various aspects of the history of the Beaux Arts, axial composition, hierarchy, repetition, and symmetry, as well as an attempt to create a static architecture of solid masses that lends the building its monumental nature. This search for monumentality is not based on the development of modern forms but seeks to interpret history, expressed in heavy, solid masses.

The modern art rooms are on the top floor. This allows them to receive natural lighting through a large skylight that filters the sun's rays.

On the next page, construction detail of skylight.

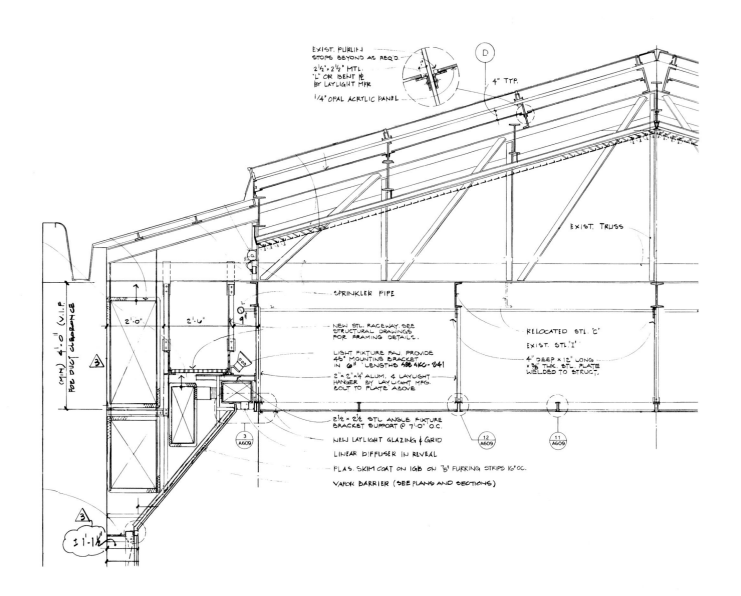

EXIST. PURLIN
STOPS BEYOND AS REQ'D.

2½" × 2½" MTL.
"L" OR BENT ℙ
BY LAYLIGHT MFR.

¼" OPAL ACRYLIC PANEL

D

4" TYP.

EXIST. TRUSS

SPRINKLER PIPE

NEW STL. RACEWAY. SEE
STRUCTURAL DRAWINGS
FOR FRAMING DETAILS.

LIGHT FIXTURE FAU PROVIDE
45° MOUNTING BRACKET
IN 6" LENGTHS SEE 4KO-841

2"×2"×4" ALUM. & LAYLIGHT
HANGER BY LAYLIGHT MFG.
BOLT TO PLATE ABOVE

2½" × 2½" STL ANGLE FIXTURE
BRACKET SUPPORT @ 7'-0" O.C.

NEW LAYLIGHT GLAZING & GRID

LINEAR DIFFUSER IN REVEAL

PLAS. SKIM COAT ON IGB ON ⅞" FURRING STRIPS 16" OC.

VAPOR BARRIER (SEE PLANS AND SECTIONS)

RELOCATED STL. "C"

EXIST. STL. "I"

4" DEEP × 12" LONG
× ⅜" THK. STL. PLATE
WELDED TO STRUCT.

(MIN) 4'-0" (V.I.F.
FOR DUCT CLEARANCE

2'-0"

2'-6"

3

3
A609

12
A609

11
A609

3

± 1'-1½"

Cross and longitudinal sections of the auditorium.

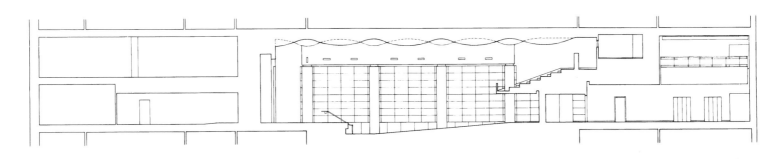

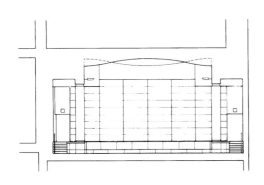

Plan of the auditorium.

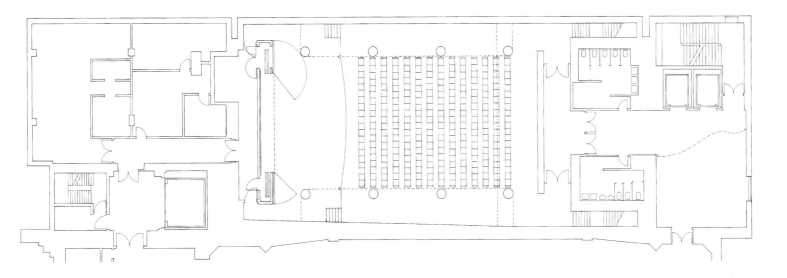

Domus

Arata Isozaki and César Portela

Near the lighthouse of Hercules, a tower erected by the Romans, is the House of Mankind, Domus, an interactive museum whose purpose is to provide a better understanding of the human body. Domus is situated atop an almost vertical cliff which drops into the sea. The site is skirted by the seafront promenade which borders the peninsula between two coves, Orzán and San Amaro.

The city council commissioned Japanese architect Arata Isozaki, in collaboration with Galician architect César Portela, to undertake the project, which takes as its point of departure the question of scale. If the project had only taken the architecture of its immediate surroundings into consideration, the solution would have had to be in keeping with the scale of the residential district around it. As it is, the building aspires to be a landmark which provides a visual connection with the Hercules lighthouse in the distance (classic in appearance now, after reinforcement work done in the 18th century), punctuating the coastline and catching the observer' s eye.

This was the basis for constructing a simple but forceful form when seen from a distance. Added considerations of the site were the climatic conditions of the Galician coast, well known for strong

Location: *La Coruña, Spain.*
Completion date: *April 1995.*
Architect: *Arata Isozaki and César Portela.*
Collaborators: *T. Tange, M. Hori, N. Ogawa, I. Peraza, A. Casares, F. Garrido, J.L. Gahona, P. Sánchez, F. José, A. Suárez.*
Photography: *Hisao Suzuki.*

The rear wall folds to expose its surfaces to the contrasts created by the sun. The entrance, which is the only opening' makes the building seem impermeable.

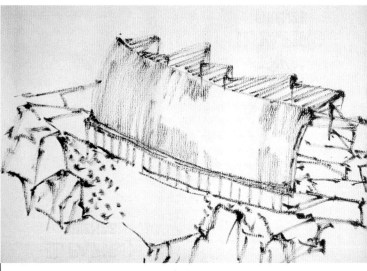

The large curved wall has rapidly become a symbol of the city.

The side façades provide the meeting point of the project's two defining walls, using the building's constructive essence as an expressive element.

The building is situated on the
former site of a quarry.

Site plan.

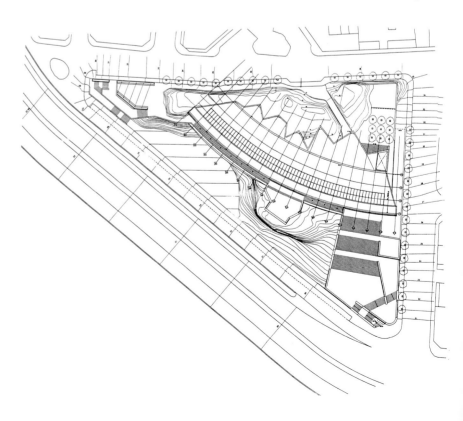

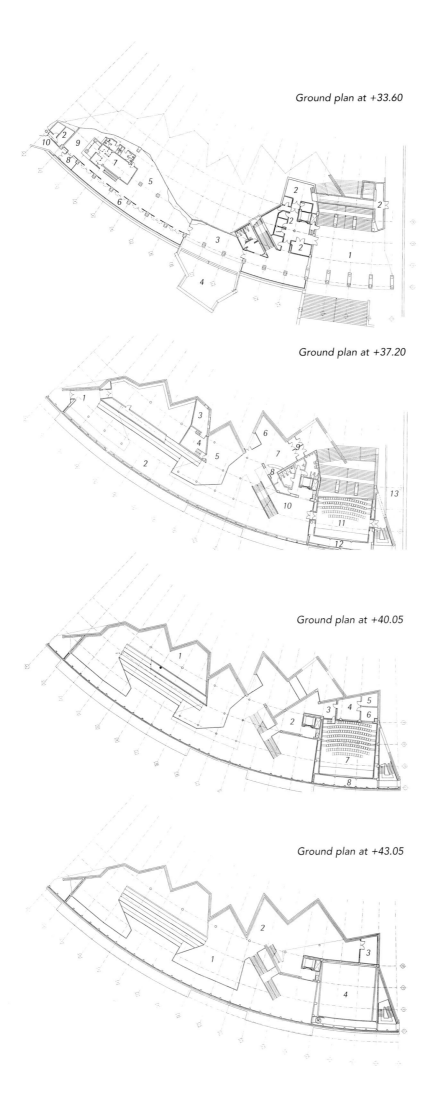

Ground plan at +33.60

1. Portico of the stairway
2. Installations
3. Outdoor picnic site
4. Picnic terrace
5. Restaurant - dining room
6. Dining room - gallery
7. Kitchens
8. Foyer
9. Bar area
10. Restaurant entrance

Ground plan at +37.20

1. Emergency exit
2. Exhibition hall A
3. Air-conditioning
4. Store room
5. Exhibition hall B
6. Display case
7. Lead-in to the foyer
8. Ticket sales
9. Main entrance
10. Foyer - Exhibition hall
11. Events hall
12. Events hall store room
13. Corridor

Ground plan at +40.05

1. Exhibition hall C
2. Audiovisuals hall
3. Lecturers' entrance
4. Projection room
5. Store room
6. Interpreters' booths
7. Events hall
8. Loudspeaker room

Ground plan at +43.05

1. Exhibition hall D
2. Temporary exhibition room
3. Air-conditioning installation
4. Space above the events hall

The exhibition space inside, lit only by the sliding skylight in the roof. This ensures adequate lighting, freeing the exhibition hall to turn its back on the sea.

The ramps running parallel to the façade compensate for the difference in level of the cliff top and reproduce the topography inside.

General view of the exhibition space.

Transversal section along axis X-10.

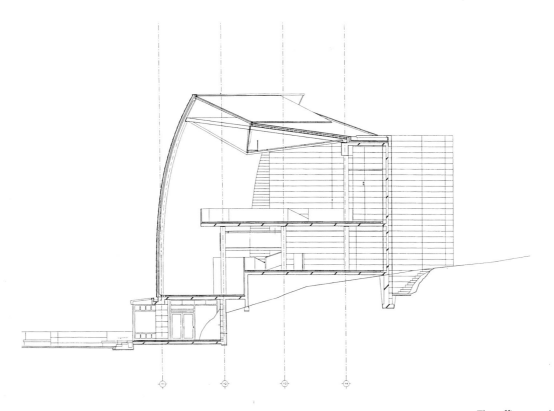

69

The offices are located on the top floor, thereby receiving the full benefit of the skylight in the roof, with vistas of the sea through the narrow strip of windows.

winds and aggressive waves. Such violent climate demands a solid building.

The response to these conditions of climate and scale took the form of a wall with very few openings, that curves as though blown by the wind. Most of the interior is designated as exhibition space and is lit from above. The building is hermetic in appearance. The two walls rise soberly, only expressing themselves in the opening of the entrance' a permeable connection from one side of the building to the other, describing a tangent inside. Visitors enter the museum via a stairway which bridges the 18-yard (17-meter) difference in height between the level of the seafront promenade and the entrance, climbing a succession of terraces with views over the Bay of Riazor.

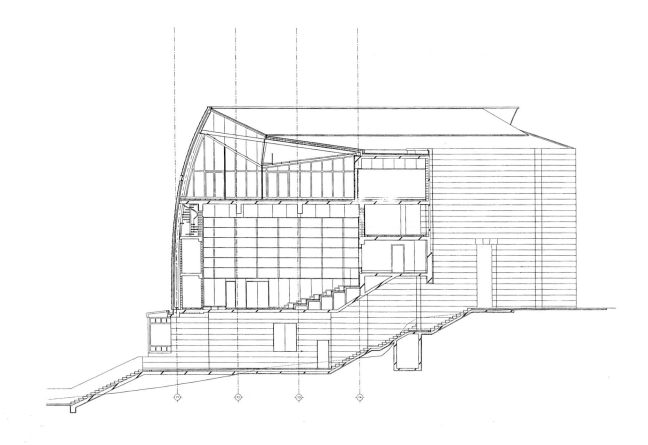

The rear of the building is a fractured granite wall reminiscent of a Japanese screen, its height and dimensions responding to the scale of the surrounding residential area. The roof, which is supported by metal trusses resting perpendicularly on the two walls, opens up into a sliding skylight for overhead lighting.

Inside is an open-plan exhibition space which adapts to the topography by means of a series of ramps linking the three levels of museum space in a linear progression. This leads into the events hall situated above the entrance from the promenade and taking advantage of the section generated by the difference in level. The hall is used for film shows and lectures which complement the exhibition.

Floor and ramp railings have been covered with the same slate used for the curved wall. Administration and study areas are situated on the top floor, beneath the skylight which extends around the perimeter. An extended restaurant is planned for the floor immediately below the exhibition hall, with a glazed terrace, similar to traditional Galician galleries, which presents a fabulous panoramic view of the bay. This is almost the only spot where visitors can look out over the sea to the horizon. The rest of the project is closed in on itself at all points, controlling vistas to focus mental concentration on the exhibitions.

The composition is simple but expressive. Overlooking the bay, a homogeneous, concave, curving wall in bluish green, resembles a gigantic wave frozen in mid-air before beating down onto the rock. On the cliff, a fractured, angular, granite wall is juxtaposed with the rock which juts irrepressibly between the two walls, a breach forged of overhead light.

The dialogue with the
topography of the cliff is taken
to its limits at the point where
the rock emerges in the
restaurant.

The events hall is a vital
part of the museum,
housing the audio-visual
area of the project.

The Guggenheim Museum

Frank O. Gehry

Bilbao is an industrial city with an important history in metallurgy. The city is divided by the Nervión River, whose banks are lined with steel mills, blast furnaces, shipyards, gigantic cranes, and warehouses. This panorama has formed an integral part of Bilbao's image since the industrial revolution. It is a harsh landscape, but also one of great visual impact and profound force.

Industrial reconversion has meant that many of these complexes have become obsolete, and they now stand idle and abandoned. Several years ago, therefore, the Basque regional government came up with a plan to revitalize the river area and renovate and convert these factory build-ings, substituting their original industrial activities with commercial, financial, and service sector uses.

The Basque authorities have tried to boost this initiative by commissioning several major projects, many on the banks of the Nervión. Among the most important of these are the metro, designed by Norman Foster, the new airport terminal by Santiago Calatrava, the Palacio de Congresos y de la Música (Convention Center and Concert Hall) by Federico Soriano, a plan for the reorganization of the Ibano-Ibarra area by César Pelli, a train-and-bus station by Michael Wildford, and the Guggenheim Museum itself.

Location: *Bilbao, Spain.*
Architect: *Frank O. Gehry.*
Design date: *1990.*
Completion date: *1997.*
Collaborators: *Randy Jefferson, Vano Haritunians, Douglas Hanson, Edwin Chan.*
Photography: *Eugeni Pons.*

Longitudinal section.

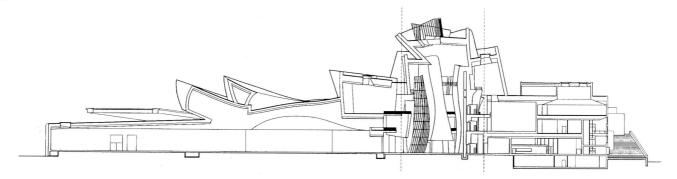

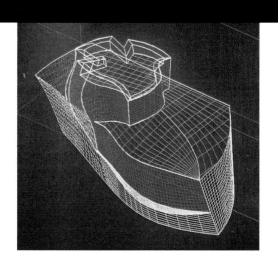

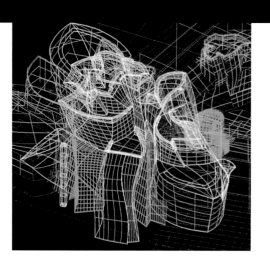

"I start with a very basic layout. In this building, for example, it's a star. There are three arms coming out of the center, and there would be a fourth if the river weren' t there." (Frank Gehry)

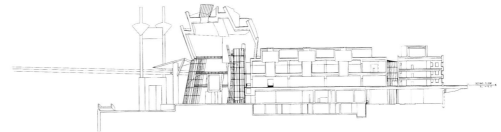

Atrium cross section.

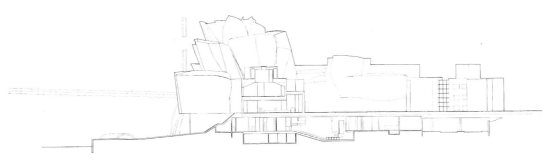

Auditorium cross section.

The curved surfaces are covered with a layer of titanium, whereas the rest of the façades are finished in limestone.

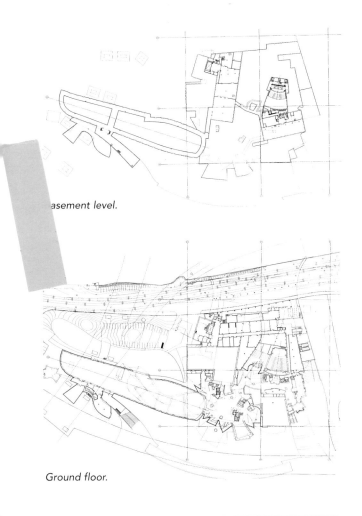

asement level.

Ground floor.

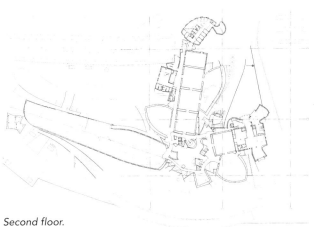

Second floor.

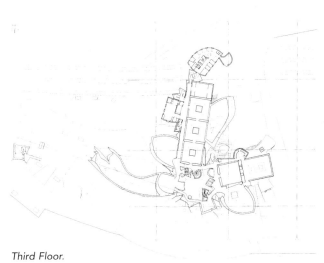

Third Floor.

According to the architect, certain scenes from Fritz Lang's film 'Metropolis' inspired the shapes in this museum.

In a restricted competition, Gehry's project was selected over projects presented by Arata Isozaki and Coop Himmelblau. Both the Basque authorities and the representatives from the Guggenheim Foundation were looking for a unique and iconoclastic building which would cause as great an impact as Frank Lloyd Wright's building for the Guggenheim Museum's headquarters in New York, and at the same time would attract international attention in the art world and become a symbol of the city. In a certain sense, the building was not only commissioned for its cultural end, but also as a symbol of the enormous metamorphosis which Bilbao is undergoing.

The museum is located on the riverbanks next to a busy suspension bridge, which Gehry took into account from the very beginning as forming part of the project. A great number of comparisons and similes can be made, but according to the architect himself, the work is based on the following themes: the film 'metropolis', by Fritz Lang, the sculptures of Brancusi, the image of a quarry, and above all, the vigor and controlled force which the city of Bilbao exudes.

The greatest influence on the final form that the building has taken, though, is of course Gehry's own style, his way of working from free sketches and models which are transferred almost literally to the computer screen, where they are mathematically analyzed in order to resolve technical and structural aspects. Thus, the museum carries the mark of Gehry above all.

The museum is composed of a large central atrium, 50 meters high (1.5 times that of the New York Guggenheim) and crowned by a "metal flower", and three wings going off to the east, the south and the west. To the north lies the river, where what would have been the fourth wing gives way to a large glass entrance.

Each of the three wings is designed to contain different types of exhibits. The permanent collection is located in the south wing, in a series of consecutive square exhibition halls. The west wing houses the collection of contemporary art, distributed in seven halls of unique and varied shapes. Temporary exhibits will be shown in a large hall (130 by 30m) which extends sinuously towards the east.

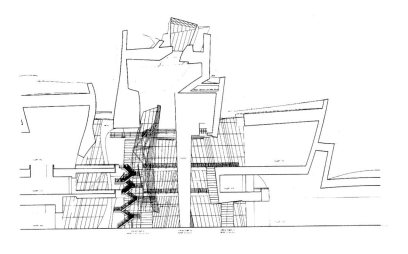

"We start on the basis of several independent elements which are combined in such a way as to harmonize with the objectives of the building. In the initial stages of my projects, this one included, there are no sculptural aspects in the proper sense of the word. We see a series of colored wooden blocks which represent the building' s functions, in this case, those of a museum. And those blocks, which have no sculptural shape, are joined together like the pieces of a puzzle. As the project advances, the technical aspect is dealt with." (Interview with Sol Alameda, El País Semanal, No. 1079)

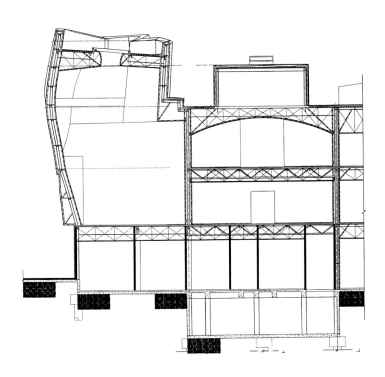

Constructive section.

The auditorium, as well as the restaurant and shops, are on the ground floor and are accessible from the plaza at the front of the museum. They have their own entrance and can therefore function independently from the museum. All the auxiliary service departments are located in the basement, which is accessed from a service road.

Arken Museum of Modern Art

Søren Robert Lund

An architectural design that excels in creating links between art and architecture is that of museums of modern art. They are spaces in which architecture interacts with art, thus giving rise to interesting, and at times ambiguous, relationships. Art enriches the formal repertory of architecture and enhances its communicative capacity. Creative proposals are tempered by the rigor of the project, while promoting freedom of expression.

The Arken Museum of Modern Art summarizes the two tendencies that evolved in Scandinavia during the 1960s, 1970s, and 1980s. One of these tendencies is expressed in Robert Lund's project, which takes up the influence of the "new empiricism" of Alvar Aalto. This architectural movement was a reaction against the excessive planning of architecture during the 1930s. It is an attempt at spontaneity, adapting buildings to traditional materials and their location. It places the habits and needs of human beings at the center of interest. It is an attempt to recover domestic comfort and an everyday feeling for texture and color. Lund, like Aalto, imbues each part of the building with an identity, creating a layout in which each function is assigned to a different element, though all are inseparably interwoven.

Location: *Arken, Denmark.*
Design date: *1993.*
Completion date: *1996.*
Architect: *Søren Robert Lund.*
Collaborators: *Helgi Thoroddson, Jorgen Erichsen, Mette Adersen, Finn Bogsted.*
Photography: *Friedrich Busam/Architekturphoto.*

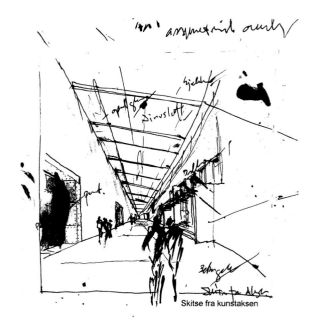

Skitse fra kunstaksen

The building stretches out over the sand dunes and vegetation like a large, horizontal volume. Lund uses the metaphor of a shipwreck as the starting point for the creative process.

The entrance, facing west, becomes narrower and narrower until it reaches almost domestic proportions, guiding the visitor in from the wide, open landscape to this intimate, "church-entrance" atmosphere.

Søren Robert Lund won the
commission in 1988, at the age of
26. The museum was opened in
1996, an eight-year interim that
saw a major transformation of the
initial project.

View of the restaurant, that
rises over the wall like a giant
crab, thrown up by the sea
onto the dunes. It is situated at
the end of one of the main
itineraries running through the
building. Thus, it becomes the
final stage of the visit.
A place to recapture images
while chatting around a table
with a view.

View of the interior patio,
or Outer Foyer as the
architect calls it. Part of the
restaurant projects through
one of the walls
surrounding the patio.

Sketch of the restaurant.

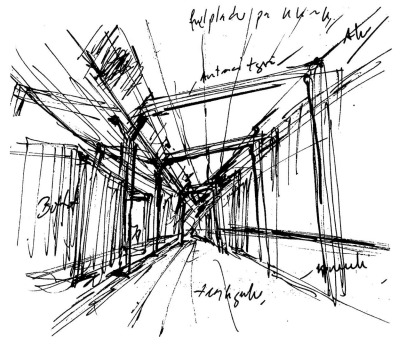

Sections.

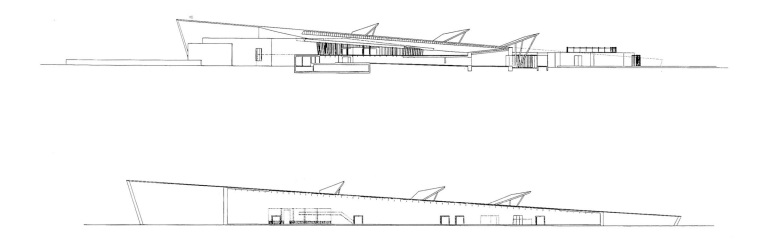

The second tendency evolving in Scandinavia, as it appears in the Arken Museum of Modern Art, is also a result of the so-called "new formal abstraction", which favors architecture that is both figurative and abstract at the same time. It is based on the interplay of forms and dynamic representation of space. The interplay of forms constitutes both the starting point and the final result. This leads to an architecture of different fragments, volumes, dynamic constructions. At the same time, it signifies a break with history and tradition, and an attempt to forget established symbols and connotations.

View of one of the main exhibition halls, with its tapered form. The desire to combine art and architecture is evident. The spaces within the building create a dramatic atmosphere that clearly conditions how the works are viewed.

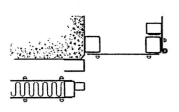

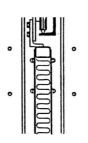

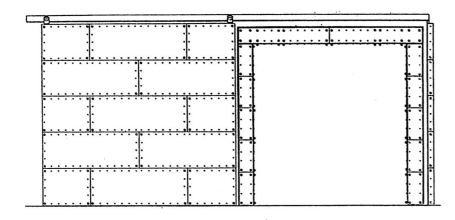

In this type of architecture, the first sketches which reflect the creative act are of special importance, as is the final result. Robert Lund uses the metaphor of a shipwreck as the starting point for the creative process, integrating it into the history of the landscape. The museum stretches out over the sand dunes, a large, horizontal volume, forming an axis that organizes the volumes of the exhibition rooms. The entrance becomes progressively smaller as the visitor advances from the wide, open landscape into a familiar, "intimate" atmosphere, like the entrance to a church.

Visitors may choose between two routes, located on the same level: the art axis leads them through a sequence of exhibition galleries with skylights and openings that look out onto the landscape. Or, via the foyer, a second route leads through space designed for complementary activities: theater rooms, projection rooms, and the restaurant.

The scale of the project is in proportion to the surrounding elements. Each space is accorded a proportion depending on its purpose, light, and acoustics. Lund was sensitive to the ruggedness of the surrounding area and chose uncovered concrete to create the building's texture. This rough skin contrasts with the façades and metal skylights to enrich the overall effect. Here, Lund reveals his great capacity for renovating forms of architectural representation. The classical system of plan, section, and elevation is consistently rejected in favor of other possibilities, such as using lines as a metaphorical language to lead us to a space brimming with images.

Each gallery offers a different situation. The form of the room, the type of lighting, the possible itineraries and the relationship between the observer and the work vary from one to another.

General plan.

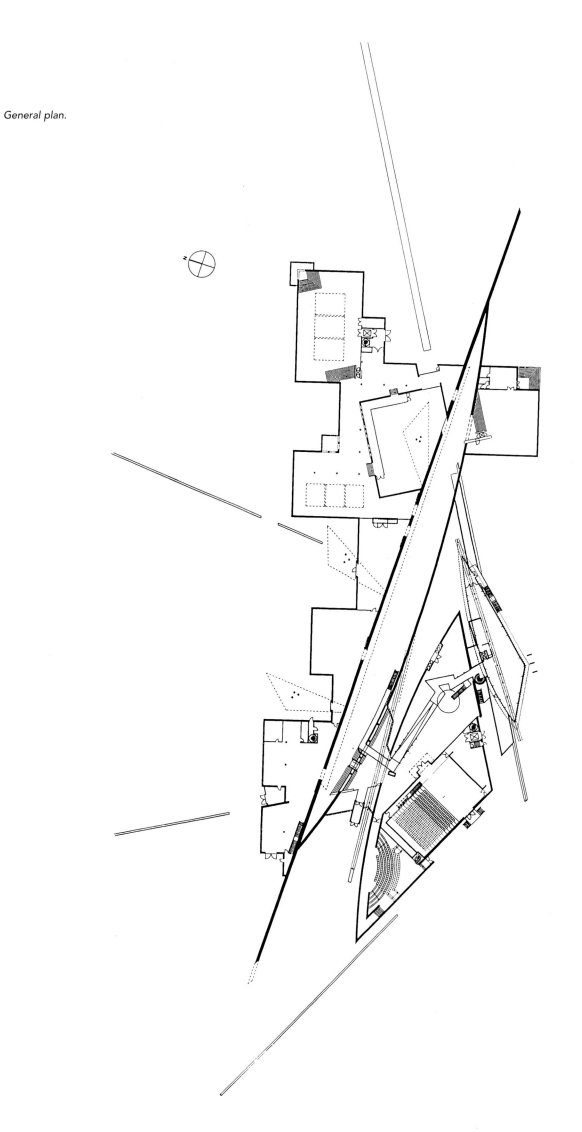

Certain elements span two
galleries and can almost be
considered two
independent works.

Natural History Museum, Rotterdam

Erik van Egeraat

The Natural History Museum is located in the so-called Museum Park in the city of Rotterdam. In 1924, when the last occupant of Villa Dijkzigt died, the Rotterdam Council bought the man sion and the surrounding area with a view to transforming it into a cultural park. Although this initiative took off strongly (the Boymnas-Van Beuningen Museum was built in 1930), interest in it waned until 1985, when the architect Rem Koolhas and the landscape architect Yves Brunnier took up the idea once again.

This marked the start of intense architectural activity in the park. During only a few years, inaugurations have included the expansion of the Boymnas-Van Beuningen by Hubert-Jan Henket, the Kunsthal by Rem Koolhas himself, the Architectural Museum by Jo Coenen, the renovation of a Villa (built in 1939 by G. W. Baas and L. Stokla) by DeWeger architects who transformed it into the Chabotmuseum, and finally, the renovation of the Natural History Museum.

The old Villa Dijkzigt, built in 1851 by F. L. Metelaar, and which housed the Natural History Museum, had finally become inadequate. Almost all the rooms were taken up with offices, workshops, and collection

Location: *Rotterdam, Holland.*
Design date: *1991.*
Completion date: *1995.*
Architect: *Erik van Egeraat.*
Collaborators: *Francine Houben, Birgit Jürgenhake, Jeroen Shipper.*
Photography: *Christian Richters.*

Views of the two entrances
to the museum: the entrance
to Villa Dijkzigt and the
addition hall, with the
connecting passageway.

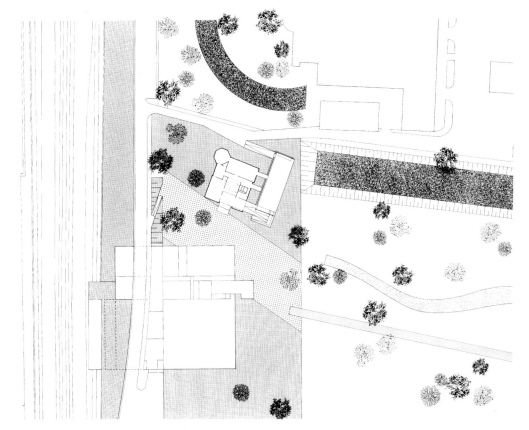

Site plan. The plan shows the
Kunsthal building, built by
Rem Koolhas (also in this
book) next to the Natural
History Museum.

depots, leaving practically no space for exhibition rooms, the permanent exhibition, temporary presentations, or visitor information services. As with many small museums founded during the 19th and early 20th centuries, this museum proved inadequate for all the activities these institutions have given rise to, such as technical services (research and conservation), or commercial areas such as cafeterias or bookstores. The initiative to renovate the old villa (catalogued as a national monument) was taken advantage of to build an annex that would solve the museum's lack of space. The new layout of the museum

included a depot in the attic for relatively light items and one in the basement for the heavier articles. The new building houses a large hall for temporary exhibits on the ground floor while the offices and library are situated on the first floor. Thus, the two main floors of the villa are devoted entirely to exhibits.

From Villa Dijkzigt, the annex is approached via a covered passageway starting at the entrance to the building. The annex has its own hall, in which a whale skeleton hangs. The annex has been designed to contrast with the old villa. The materials, shape, and technology

On the previous page, the east façade of the addition. On this page, the north façade. These façades do not follow the traditional design of a wall in which windows are opened up. Rather, it is a series of overlapping "skins," each made of a different material. Thus, glass not only forms the windows but also entire facings, even when the concrete wall is still visible behind it.

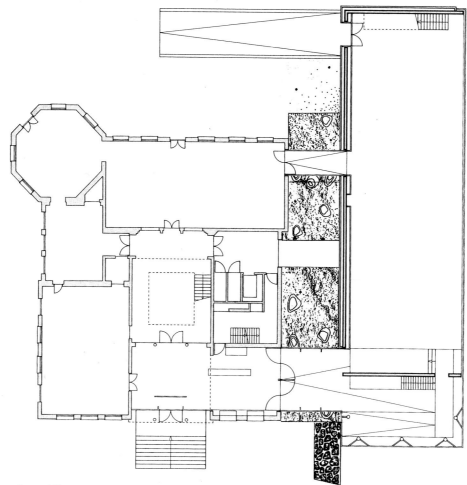

Ground floor.

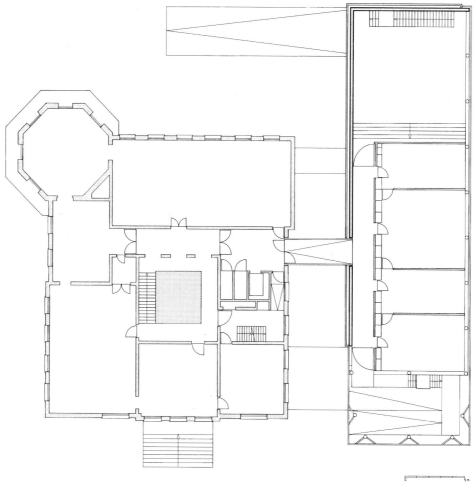

First floor.

View of one of the renovated rooms of the old museum.

applied are all totally different to those used for the main museum building. These two buildings are separated by an elongated garden, inspired by Japanese models. This addition is a simple, rectangular building. According to van Egeraat the façade has been designed as a series of different "skins." The first is made of concrete and encloses the exhibit space. The second, made of glass, acts as a membrane around the concrete skin. The third skin is brick and stands between the south and west façades. This serves to prevent too much sunlight from reaching the glass.

If the visitors approach the museum from the park, the first image they encounter is the hall with a whale suspended in the air, standing out against the concrete wall as if it were in an enormous glass fish-tank. The view from the dike, however, is dominated by the old villa which almost completely conceals the addition.

Different views of the concrete wall

that separates the addition hall from

the temporary exhibit area.

The temporary exhibit area is a space measuring approximately 250 square meters. Sparse, unsettling, and evocative elements are used. A large, single window illuminates the hall. This window, however, is situated at floor level, well below eye-level, so that the normal view of the exterior is directed toward the lawn surrounding the building and the lower section of the tree trunks. The light reflects off the concrete floor. Artificial points of light form a grid-pattern embedded in the floor and walls. The ceiling has no lights, however. Finally, a staircase appears on the ceiling as if ceiling and floor had changed places.

At the end of the hall, a staircase connects this area with the library, which is open to the public.

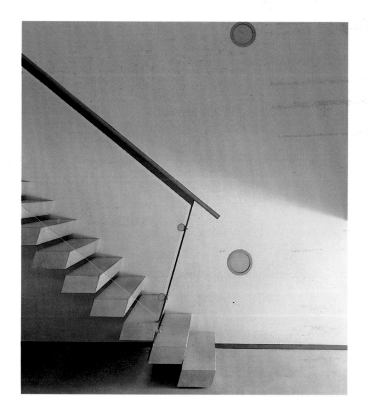

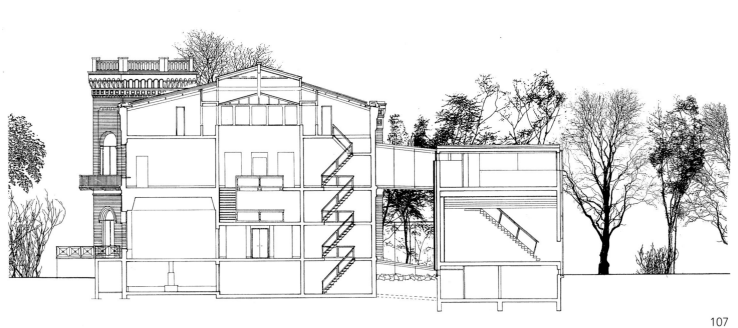

The Old Provence Research Institute

Henri E. Ciriani

The building designed by Henri Ciriani is located at the foot of the remains of an old Roman stadium, next to the river on a small peninsula formed by a canal. Of the stadium, only its shape and a small section of the foundations are visible. It had become a kind of no-man's land, a void between the old city and the new neighborhoods. The museum itself is a type of sign- highlighting the ruins and linking the old city to the new. The building resembles the setting for a day's celebrations in the stadium. The easily-identifiable shape of a triangle was chosen for the form of the building while a vivid blue was used for the façades. Ciriani has said that the image of the building was designed as a type of sign.

The city of Arles already possessed many buildings that were circular or square in shape. The triangle was chosen to complete this set of forms. The composition of each façade depends on its orientation. The façade looking onto the canal lock, facing south, is completely hermetic; the one overlooking the river has a lower section made of glass and a structure of walls and lintels, like a brille-soleil; and lastly,

Location: *Arles, France.*
Completion date: *1995.*
Architect: *Henri Ciriani.*
Collaborators: *Jacques Bajolle, Jacky Nicholas.*
Photography: *Jean-Marie Monthiers.*

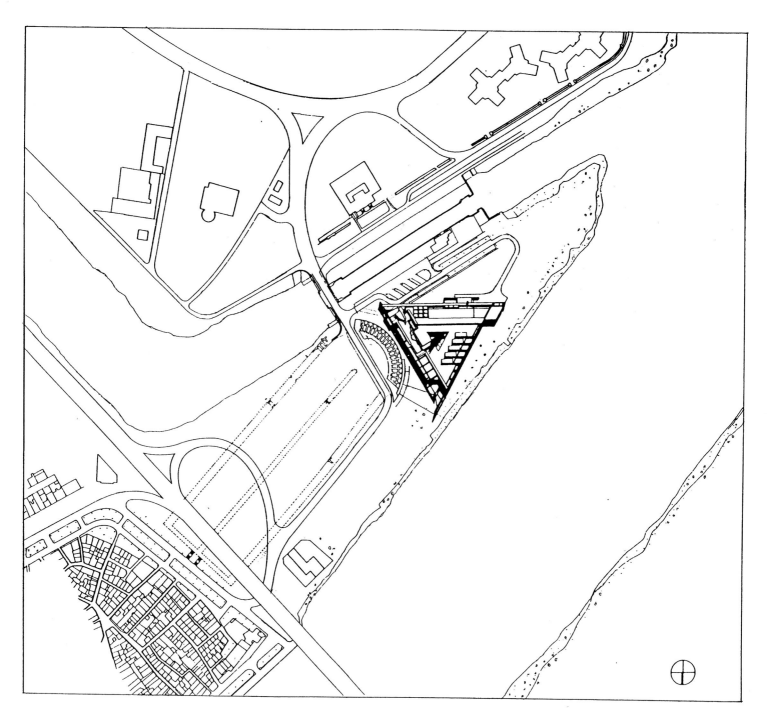

Site plan.

the main façade, facing the stadium and the old city, offers an interplay of volumes, openings, and projections.

The types of object on exhibit in the museum, such as mosaics, sculptures, vessels, are best displayed at floor level. At the same time, the museum program called for two types of itinerary: one long and another short. The spatial solution invented by Ciriani was to create a loop having the same starting and finishing point –the hall– but with sections of differing width, enabling the visitor to move quickly through the rooms or linger.

Additionally, in the larger exhibit rooms, the mosaics can be situated on the floor, while in the narrower ones, vitrines or panels are displayed.

The center of the loop is a triangular patio through which light enters the rooms. A monumental, concrete staircase with a triangular profile connects the patio with the roof-garden. At the same time, the staircase prevents visitors from looking from one room into another.

In Ciriani's own words, the hall is a true urban interior, and this explains the overall organization of the building. It provides

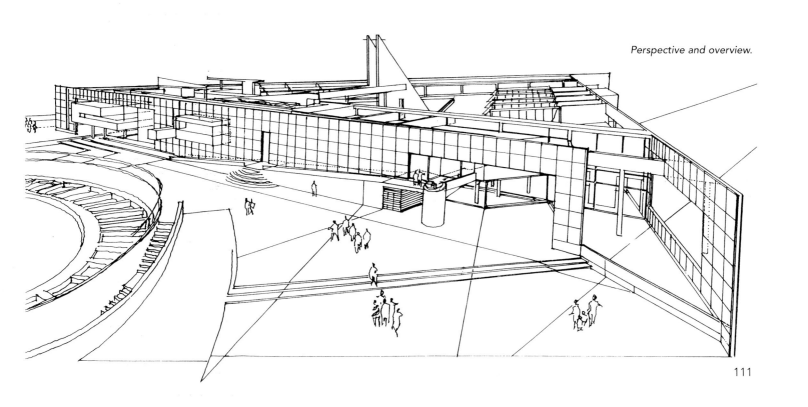

Perspective and overview.

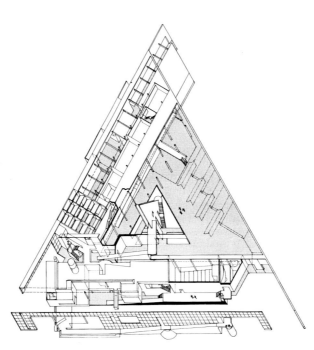

Although the form of the building is a perfect triangle, Henri Ciriani has chosen to round off the angles. The entrance is located on the east vertex. According to the architect, "The removal of the angles creates a helix which hinges on the belvedere staircase of the central patio."

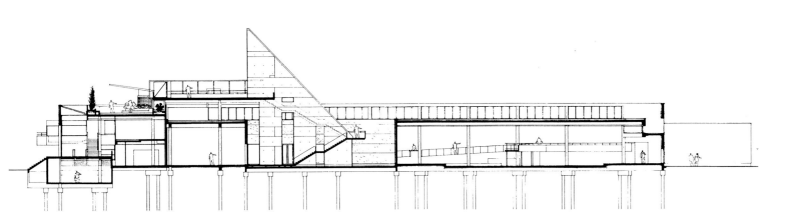

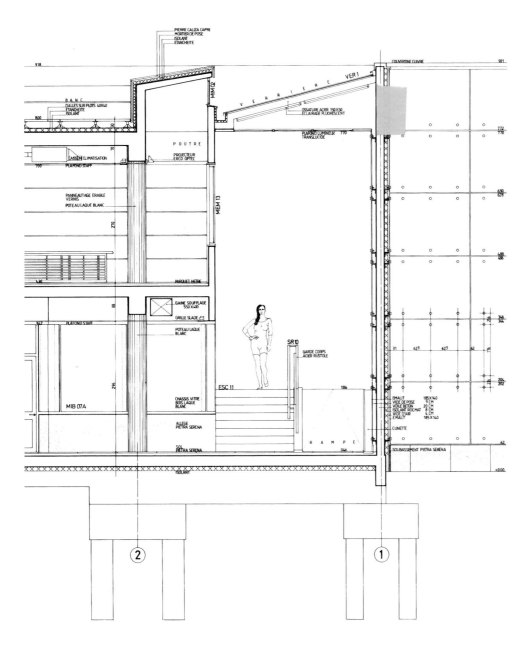

Labels in the drawing:

PIERRE CALIZA CAPRI
MORTIER DE POSE
ISOLANT
ÉTANCHEITE

918
COUVERTINE CUIVRE
921

VER 1

VERRIERE

BANC
DALLES SUR PLOTS 40X60
ÉTANCHEITE
ISOLANT
800

MIM 02

OSSATURE ACIER 150 X50
ÉCLAIRAGE FLUORESCENT

772
770

POUTRE

PLAFOND LUMINEUX
TRANSLUCIDE
770

CAISSON CLIMATISATION
PLAFOND STAFF
700

PROJECTEUR
ERCO OPTEC

630
628

PANNEAUTAGE ÉRABLE
VERNIS
POTEAU LAQUÉ BLANC

MEM 13

270

480
486

PARQUET HÊTRE

GAINE SOUFFLAGE
550 X400

GRILLE SLADE

346
342

PLAFOND STAFF

POTEAU LAQUÉ
BLANC

SR10

GARDE CORPS
ACIER RUSTOLE

31   623   623   62

MIB 07A

ESC 11

CHASSIS VITRÉ
BOIS LAQUÉ
BLANC

206
202

186

RAMPE

EMALIT   185 X 140
VIDE DE POSE   9 CM
VOILE BÉTON   20 CM
ISOLANT ROCMAT   8 CM
VIDE D'AIR   6 CM
EMALIT   185 X 140

ALLÈGE
PIETRA SERENA

046

CUNETTE

SOL
PIETRA SERENA

SOUBASSEMENT PIETRA SERENA
62

+000

ISOLANT

② ①

A construction detail of the gallery running parallel to the façade designed to inform the visitors. The lighting is provided by a zenithal skylight.

access to the permanent exhibition rooms as well as to the two, independent wings which, in addition to the museum, form the Old Provence Research Institute.

The first wing is organized along the main façade. It includes the tourist information center, the documentation department, educational services, conference room, and cafeteria. A longitudinal gallery, located just behind the façade and illuminated by a long skylight, connects the two spaces.

The second wing has a strictly scientific function. Running along the south façade are the photographic laboratory and others containing glass pieces, mosaics and bronze, the center of archeological studies, the curator' s department, the store- house, services department and the loading and unloading bay.

The exhibition rooms are paved with gray-colored stone; the structure, a network of round pillars, is made of white cement; the roof and the enclosure walls are plastered and painted white. Color is reserved for the objects on display, for the panels, and the furniture. Ciriani works with light. In the roof of the main room he creates a series of skylights facing north. Next to the façade, a series of concrete planes that reflect the light that enters through the windows. There is an ambiguous relationship between the interior and the exterior. The lighting is never direct,

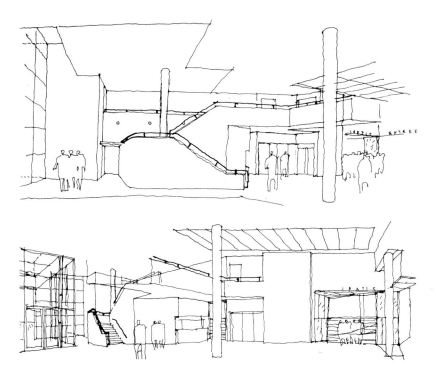

Sketches and views of the vestibule.

115

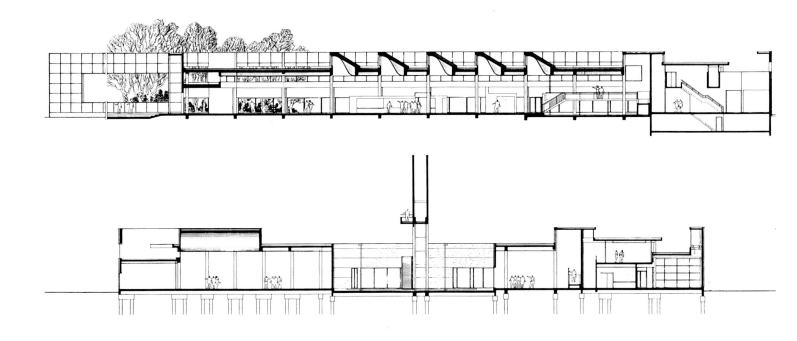

but enters through skylights, interior patios, or brille-soleil structures. Light is controlled and filtered so as to illumi-nate each room in a different manner, to establish the itinerary according to the vary- ing intensities of the light and so that light is perceived by the visitors as an essential part of the museum.

During the day, the openings in the enclosure walls create a homogenous atmosphere; while at night, the artificial lighting produces a theater-like effect. Spotlights illuminate the scene, turning the unsuspecting visitors into actors surrounded by images from another age.

The blue panes of glass in the façade reflect the sky. This material lends the façade the appearance of a mirage in which the continuous movement of the clouds is reflected. Ciriani sees this as a sign that reveals how the old Roman town of Arles lives on in the spirit of today's residents and in the future of the city.

The depth of the exhibition rooms acts as a counterbalance to the loop-shaped itinerary. Thus, a visitor entering for a short visit finds the main pieces in the foreground while the mid-ground and the rooms at the end contain other pieces that would make up part of a longer visit.

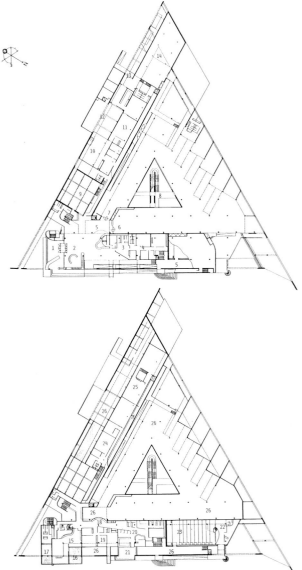

1. Entrance

2. Hall

3. Children's workshop

4. Guides' school

5. Gallery

6. Entrance to permanent exhibition

7. Exit from permanent exhibition

8. Patio and access to roof garden

9. Temporary exhibition

10. Workshop

11. Laboratories

12. Workshops' corridor

13. Service area

14. Storehouse

15. Cafeteria

16. Terrace

17. Personnel room

18. Waiting room

19. Offices

20. Library and archive

21. Reading room

22. Auditorium

23. Orchestra

24. Archeology school

25. Storehouse

26. Empty space

Kunsthal

Rem Koolhaas

"Let us free architecture from responsibilities it can no longer assume and aggressively explore this newly acquired freedom."

Koolhaas resorts to an arbitrary, irrational, underground force, a force approaching surrealism, in order to establish his method of work. The aim is to create an artificial state of unconsciousness. "I have always believed in uncertainty," says the architect. "In order to be fully convinced of something, one needs to feel a profound abhorrence for almost everything else. Thus, in certain projects, it is essential to explore our phobias to reinforce our convictions."

A primordial aim drives all Koolhaas' work, from his writing to his projects and buildings. This aim shapes his decisions on every scale, from the domestic to the urban, from the diagram to the detail. This aim is to discover the true cooperation that can exist between architecture and freedom. To eliminate any trace of unjustified authority, of unnecessary domination or conventionalism, Koolhaas "stabs" the project "to reveal the underlying nerves," thus reducing his expectations. This reduction furnishes him with the crucial strategy he uses in all his projects to transform a design into an instrument of freedom.

Location: *Rotterdam, Holanda.*
Design date: *1987.*
Completion date: *1992.*
Collaborators: *Fuminori Hoshino, Tony Adams, Isaac Batenburg, Leo van Immerzeel, Herman Jacobs, Edu Arroyo, Jim Njoo, Marc Peeters, Ron Steiner, Jeroen Thomas y Patrcia Blaisse (Interiors and garden).*
Photography: *LOCK IMAGES.*

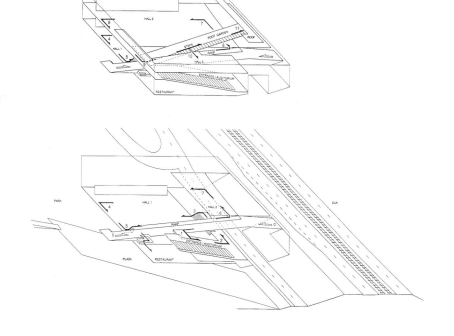

Two aspects of the roof.

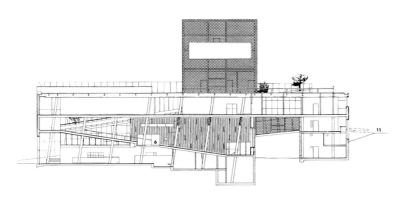

Longitudinal section of the auditorium.

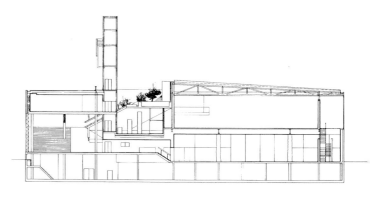

Cross section.

View of the bar from the exterior.

Longitudinal section of the exhibition rooms.

Longitudinal section of the entrance ramp.

Koolhaas gives a hedonistic,
libertarian interpretation to
the architecture of the
Modern Movement as it
includes their proposals but
does not seek to recover their
rational, order-orientated
criteria. Koolhaas is conscious
that historical events have
mercilessly destroyed this
supposed order.

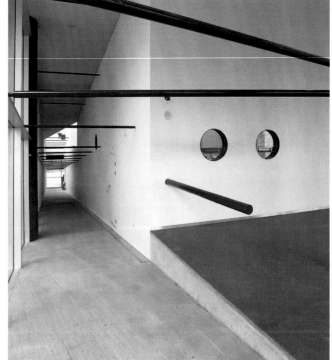

Located between the heavy traffic of an avenue and an area that borders the Museum Park, Rotterdam's Kunsthal finds itself in a dual situation. One of the façades faces onto the park, a traditional context of tranquillity and contemplation, while the other, located on a higher level, faces the massive volume of the dike and the promenade running along the top.

The building's layout is that of a continuous circuit. A pedestrian ramp divides it longitudinally, linking the walk and the park. The outer section, open to the public, becomes an integral part of the inner itinerary of the art gallery. Parallel to this walk is a second ramp and, where the two ramps meet, the main entrance to the first room.

This museum is a coherent synthesis of several, well-known, modern precedents, the most obvious of which is the National

Gallery by Mies van der Rohe in Berlin.
Here visitors leave the street and climb up
a staircase before arriving at an enormous
empty concrete plinth which looks over
the entire area. This ascension to a higher
plane harks back to the entrances to
Renaissance churches where the stairs

would lead the parishioners upward, from the profane to the sacred. After entering the building and walking through the galleries, visitors again find themselves outside on a kind of plinth, although very different to that of Mies' ; this one projects from the building at street level and appears to connect with it. This conclusion to the visit creates a situation of ambiguity and surprise, as it appears to situate visitors in the midst of the traffic.

The relationship the museum has with the city is one of discerning fascination. The Kunsthal has been described as "an intentional exploitation of penetration." The building becomes a disorganized body, capable of restructuring itself, or letting itself be traversed by different currents, flowing in different directions, such as the pedestrian and street traffic. Space is created by the various itineraries and the pace is modified by the various ways in which these directions interconnect.

In this project, the structural strategy employed is also a means of disarticulating space. The elimination of the structural mesh excludes metrical references and thereby the possibility of a formal code. It uses functionally specialized structures within a single volume. The leaning columns defy the laws of gravity and align themselves with the project' s topography: a radical declaration of freedom and independence from the natural order of things. Koolhaas seeks to create new territories which, far from regulating and controlling, open up an amoral, experimental space in which certain concepts can unfold in any direction.

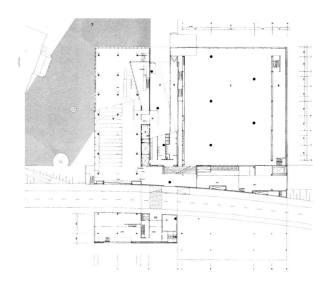

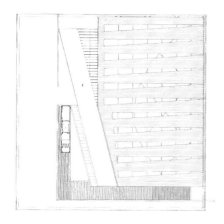

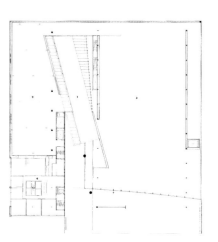

Ground floor.

Second floor.

Third floor.

Roof.

View of the auditorium.

Natural History Museum, London Primates Gallery and Earth Galleries

Terry Pawson/Keith Williams

The Natural History Museum was built from 1873-1881 in the Romanesque style by Alfred Waterhouse. Adjacent to the museum are the Geological Museum and the Science Museum, both built in the neo-Classical style during the early decades of the 20th century by the Ministry of Works.

In recent years, many of the galleries have been renovated to adapt them to current feelings on exhibition areas; areas where objects are not displayed in static form, but which offer itineraries through which the explicative panels, computer screens, and the almost dramatic atmosphere of the area invite the visitor to participate. The ultimate aim, therefore, is not merely to classify and divulge the contents but to incorporate the museum into the type of place where people will readily spend their leisure time.

In the case of the Natural History Museum, this renovating process was not carried out by a single architect, as was the Louvre, but by four. Thus, Ian Ritchie remodeled the Ecology Gallery, David Chipperfield the Plant Gallery, and Ron Herron the Dinosaur Gallery. Pawson and Williams were responsible for the Primates Gallery and the redevelopment of the Geological Museum.

Location: *London, England.*
Design date: *1996.*
Architect: *Terry Pawson, Keith Williams.*
Collaborators: *Alain Bacon, Jeremy Browne, Richard Browne, David Thompson.*
Photography: *Chris Gascoigne, Nathan Willcock.*

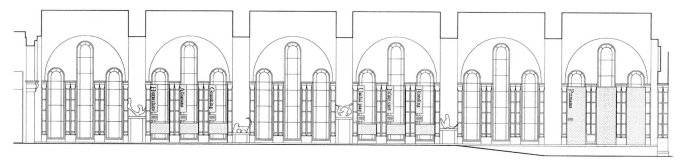

Elevation of the Primates Gallery.

The Primates Gallery is situated on the first floor western balcony of the main hall. It is reached by a monumental flight of steps rising up from the hall. It is a long, narrow space, a corridor 36 m in length, with a high ceiling. On one side is a series of stained glass windows while on the other a stone balustrade looks over the main hall.

The Gallery still clearly follows the order established by Alfred Waterhouse, in which the same, roughly square module is repeated. Each of these modules is bounded on either side by pilasters

Detail of windows. The translucent glass signs are a reinterpretation of the stained glass windows.

which form the framework for three windows or arches. The original space designed by Waterhouse undoubtedly produced a powerful, solid image: columns, moldings, arches, the light entering through the stained glass windows, the stone walls, vaults, and so on. The architects have respected, yet reinterpreted, the way the original gallery used space, color, and light.

The main modification has been to raise the deck on the side opposite the balustrade, which not only creates space for the electrical cabling and computer connections but, more importantly, creates two different levels that enrich and

enhance the area. The materials used, bronze, glass and stone, evoke the atmosphere, the light, and color of the original space. The color and the positioning of the new display elements, however, are clearly independent from the original.

The Geological Museum is located in the 1935 building, with its neo-Classical façades and its interior that has a quasi-industrial character. The ground floor of the building is practically rectangular, with an atrium in the center three floors in height, 40 m in length, and 12 m in width, roofed by a glazed barrel vault. A ring of three floors, with 9 m wide exhibition gal-

Overall plan of the Gallery.

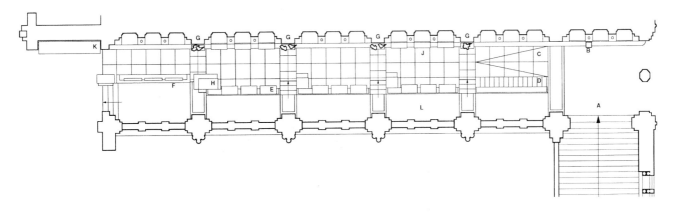

Different views of the new hall of the Geological Museum, enlarged by Pawson and Williams. Display cases containing prehistoric animals have been mounted over the information desks and ticket area.

leries housing the exhibition rooms, encircles the atrium. Until recently, the museum hosted few visitors, despite its importance. The contents were displayed in traditional manner, in conventional display cases. Recent attempts to make it more interactive had not succeeded, and it was not until Pawson and Williams' proposal that the need to modernize its image to attract more public was addressed.

The entrance hall has been completely remodeled, enlarging its volume and height. The atrium that previously opened onto the side galleries has been sheathed with slate panels turning it into a lofty, dramatic, top-lit space. A central escalator runs from the atrium toward the upper gallery, passing through a 10-meter-diameter steel globe, an allegorical representation of the Earth that slowly rotates as people travel up through it.

In contrast to this dramatic "black box," the side galleries have been developed as "white boxes," a host space for other designers to work freely on each exhibition.

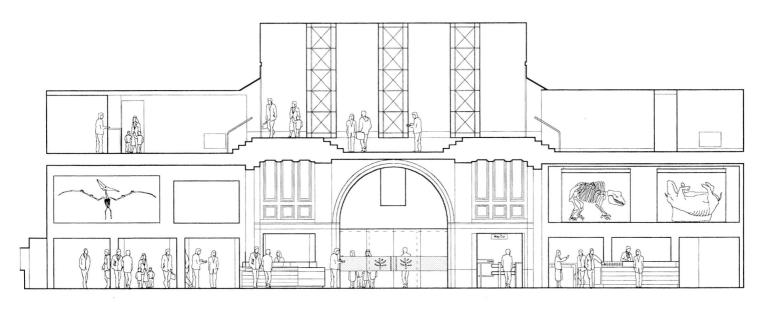

General elevation of the Hall.

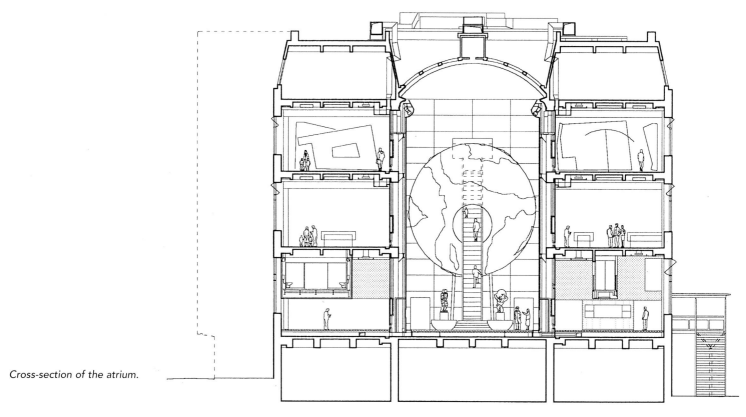

Cross-section of the atrium.

Detail of the stairs.

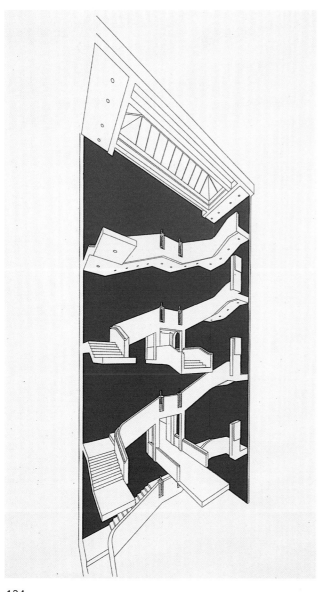

View of the staircase rising from the hall, on the ground floor, to the atrium. The escalator to the atrium and the steel globe are visible in the background.

Entrance to the foyer.

General plan.

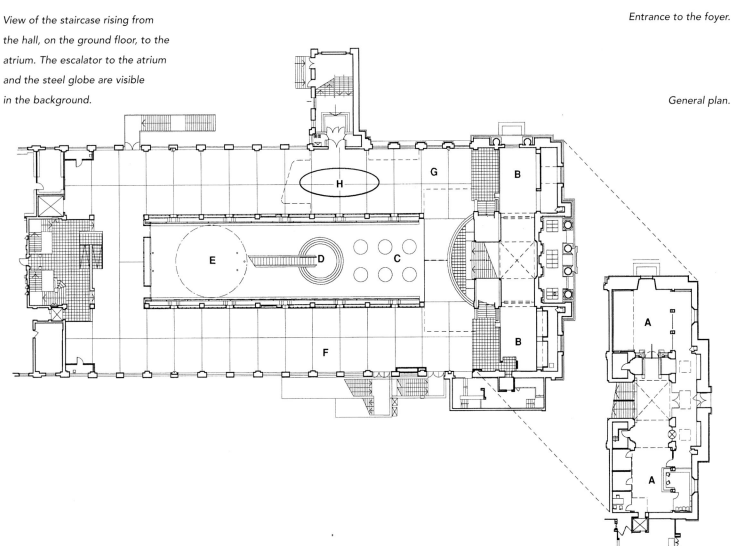

Chiado Museum

Jean-Michel Wilmotte

Not far from Santa Justa, next to Rua Garret in the very heart of Chiado, which was devastated by a fire on 25th August 1988, the French architect Jean-Michel Wilmotte has rebuilt the old Museum of Contemporary Art which, although still dedicated to divulging Portuguese art of the past two centuries, has now adopted the name Chiado Museum.

This reconstruction of the museum has brought with it an enlargement: several old buildings adjacent to the old Museum of Contemporary Art have been integrated into the exhibition complex.

These neighboring buildings include the Franciscan convent from the 13th century, which was destroyed and rebuilt after the earthquake in the 18th century, and several of the old buildings of the School of Fine Arts. Wilmotte has endeavored to lend unity to this heterogenous collection while placing special emphasis on conserving the elements characteristic to each of these old buildings and, in particular, the brick arches and vaults of the convent's bakery.

Thus, the final project is based on an ongoing dialogue between the original

Location: *Lisbon, Portugal.*
Completion date: *1994.*
Architect: *Jean-Michel Wilmotte.*
Collaborators: *Alain Desmarchelier, Denis Boyer-Gibaud, Yvan Masson.*
Photography: *Gregori Civera.*

Whereas as in the past the entrance to the museum led through the garden, the project for rebuilding and enlargement has relocated it in the large, vaulted room.

View of the courtyard. The garden is designed using straight lines, both horizontally and for the façades: the fountain, staircase, flowerbeds, large windows and lattice-work complete a perfectly geometric composition.

Floor and sections. The view shows how the museum has the composition of a jigsaw puzzle, fitting together the different rooms surrounding the courtyard and which are the result of works carried out at various times.

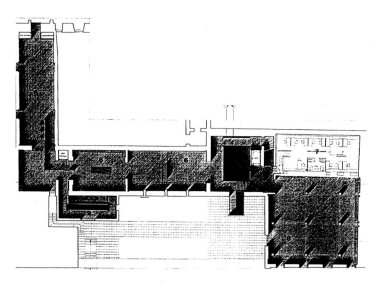

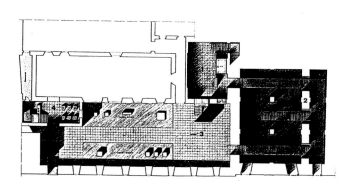

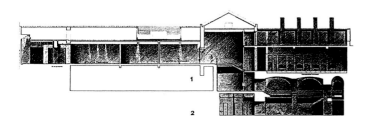

remains of the building and the new materials employed. For Wilmotte, it was important that visitors realize that the museum rooms now occupy spaces that in the past were put to different purposes.

In one way, this series of different atmospheres, each with its own, strong personality, has a considerable influence on the scale of the museum, or rather, on the way the visitors walking around the rooms perceive it. There are no large rooms, no enormous hallways, but rather a pervading atmosphere that transmits a

The enlarged museum has
2700 square meters of
exhibition rooms.
The collection includes
Portuguese paintings from
1850 to 1950.

View of the hall situated in
the old bakery of the
Franciscan convent.

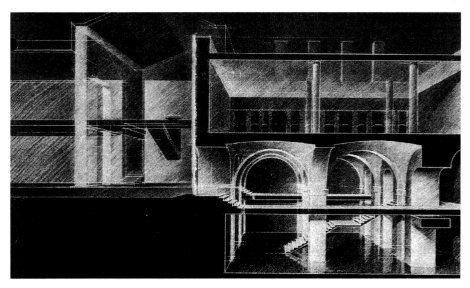

The French government proposed and funded this restoration of the museum in a gesture of solidarity with local authorities and within the framework of similar works in Chiado.

One of the elements to which Jean-Michel Wilmotte paid most attention was lighting. In almost all the exhibition rooms, artificial light is combined with natural light (entering through the skylights with ultraviolet filters).

sensation of intimacy, peace, and recollection. Visitors are not overwhelmed with the feeling of witnessing a great cultural event, but rather they enjoy the pleasure of contemplating works undistorted by their reputation.

This feeling is, in large part, intensified by the interior garden, used for exhibiting sculptures, and separated from the street by a wall. Indeed, one of Jean-Michel Wilmotte's greatest achievements has been to fully assimilate the spirit and the atmosphere of a district with so strong a character as Chiado. All the museum spaces maintain the human scale of the buildings, side-streets, and squares that surround them; and despite being newly built, a certain melancholy tendency can already be noted in the garden and several of the rooms.

Stiklestad Cultural Center

Jens Petter Askim

On 29th July 1030, the battle of Stiklestad took place. That was one of the most important events in Norwegian history and is considered as marking the transition from the Age of the Vikings to the Middle Ages. Despite King Olaf's defeat by the local chiefs, his martyrdom and death paradoxically came to signify the achievement of his main goals: the Christianization and unification of Norway. Saint Olaf is today one of the most popular figures in Scandinavia, and Stiklestad the destination for his pilgrims.

In accordance with this, the museum designed by Jens Petter Askim has several purposes. It is intended to commemorate the battle of Stiklestad and the figure of Saint Olaf and to explain the consequences and causes of that historical event. The museum ought also to present Viking culture prior to Saint Olaf, the scenes and remains of the decisive battle, and the historical changes that have affected the country since that time. Finally, the Viking Cultural Center is intended to be a meeting place for carrying out activities and welcoming pilgrims who, before the museum was built, would stay in the nearby town of Trondheim or on the site of the battle itself.

Location: *Stiklestad, Norway.*
Design date: *1985.*
Completion date: *1992.*
Architect: *Jens Petter Askim, Sven Hartvig.*
Photography: *Bard Ginnes, Jens Petter Askim.*

The construction of the museum, as with almost all major works in Scandinavia, was the subject of a public contest that drew much attention. The winning project, by Jens Petter Askim and Sven Hartvig, was presented under the title, There Were People on Every Path.

The building is a conceptually modern work, showing great concern for the landscape, yet designed in accordance with the canons of "common architecture." Thus, the double-pitched roofs and the wall that encloses the south side of the courtyard, the bridges, the earthen bank on which the building stands, or the

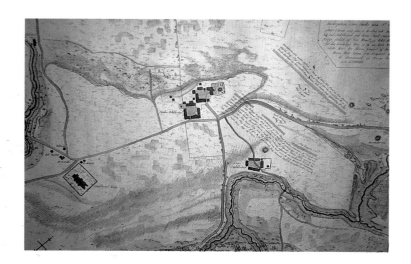

Preliminary.

146

Images taken of the museum from the meadow. The curved wall standing out from the slope, the double-pitched roofs hanging over the shade; the inner courtyard with its passageways and balconies. These are powerful images that are not readily classifiable.

Statue of Saint Olaf holding a crucifix, the forerunner of Christianity in Norway.

Detail of one of the side
façades.

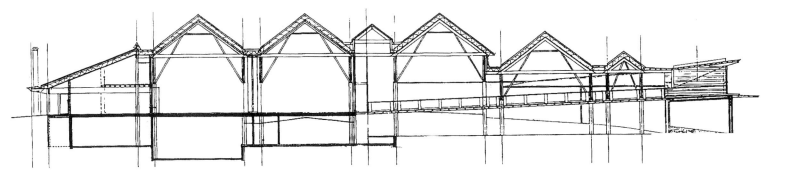

The open amphitheater next to the museum, built on a gentle slope.

structure itself take their inspiration from simple, traditional elements.

The architects' intention was, first, that the building should blend into the landscape, merging with the type of buildings in the vicinity of Stiklestad; and second, that the architectural setting should prepare visitors for the scenes and archeological treasures that await them inside the museum.

The main space within the museum is the courtyard. This is intended to be a multi-use center. It is bounded to the south side by a circular, stone hallway where archaeological pieces are on display and scenes are shown from the battle of Stiklestad.

The entire museum is covered by a series of double-pitched roofs linking these open and closed spaces. The architects strove to create a variety of different situations in which the privacy of the rooms and the relationship established between the different spaces may vary depending on the activities taking place. The balconies on the first floor, the tree-like form of the pillars (a concrete base from which spring up a row of metal pillars that support the roof), the shaded courtyard, like a leafy wood are all elements which help to reinforce the landscaped effect of the museum.

The building designed by Askim eschews picturesque images and themes to create an architecture that is complex yet lyrical at the same time.

View of one of the exhibition rooms. Unlike the theater or the auditorium, the permanent exhibition spaces are located in an almost hermetically closed corridor in which artificial, almost theater-like lighting is of major importance for lending greater dramatism to the objects and scenes on display.

Working model.

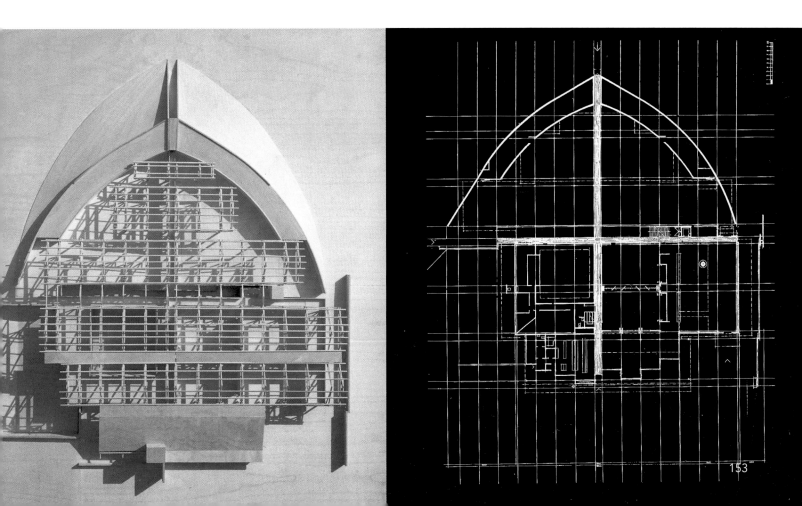

Okazaki Art and Historical Museum

Akira Kuryu

After the Second World War in Japan, a new type of garden emerged that differed from the design of the traditional Japanese garden. These new gardens were created in response to the demands of a new type of client and became part of the standard architecture of administrative buildings, cultural venues, museums, office buildings, and public squares.

The new prototype no longer sought to imitate nature, but to declare the artist's desire to express his or her individuality. These innovative artists, whose influences are international, no longer confine themselves to Japanese traditions. On the contrary, their compositions are generally abstract and often hardly resemble gardens, but sculptures to be walked through. In them we discover the dualism between humanity and nature, hitherto unknown in Japan. The desire to impose on nature the supposedly independent will of humanity.

The Okazaki Art and Historical Museum is located in the city's Central Park. It is surrounded by vegetation and stands on a terrain sloping gently down to a pond. The architect Akira Kuryu has sought to combine both Eastern and Western traditions. On one hand, we see the desire to share

Location: *Okazaki, Aichi, Japan.*
Design date: *1992.*
Completion date: *1996.*
Architect: *Akira Kuryu.*
Collaborators: *Toshihiko Kimura + Kimura (construction), Hanawa (construction), Sogo (mechanics),* PLACEMEDIA *(Land scape architecture), Fujie Kuzuko Atelier (furniture).*
Photography: *Nacasa & Partners.*

the concept of individualism with the visitors, and on the other, to summon the powers of nature to transmit a sensation of equilibrium and spiritual harmony.

Kuryu has combined the layouts of the park and of the building. Two axes extend like natural surfaces, one water, the other wind, guiding us away from the world of the city and cement and into the museum. Modern windmills lined up like metallic trees, fountains of tiny droplets, waterfalls, and a steam all create a living space conducive to preparing the visitor's senses for reflection.

The Okazaki Museum is conceived as a space for recreation and relaxation. Museums in Japan have long been looked upon as places for contemplative people who would devote their lives to studying and cultivating the spirit. The West has

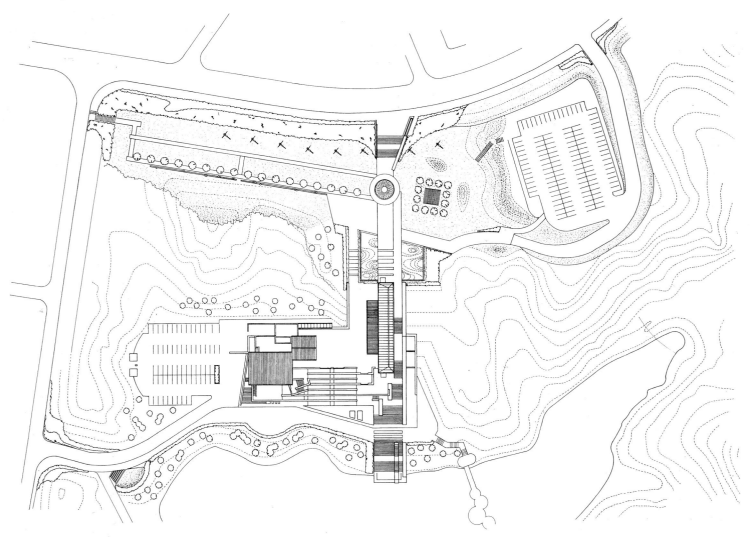

General plan.

The windmills, the leaves of the trees being
stirred by the wind, the ever-changing mist,
the flowing water: all create a dynamic
universe against a static landscape. Visitors
participate in this dual image.

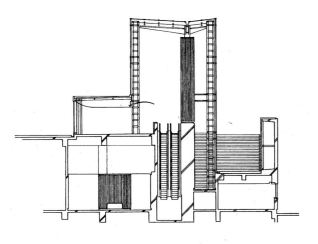

Cross section of the glass volume.

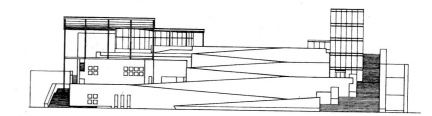

Elevation from pond.

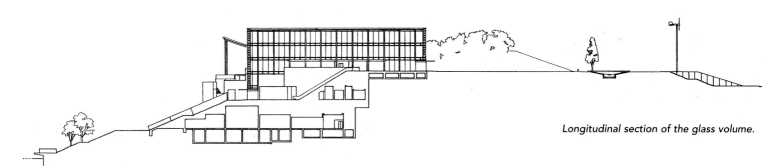

Longitudinal section of the glass volume.

Where the wind and water axes meet,
Fujiko Nakaya has designed a sculpture
from which steam emerges.

The building is terraced, following the sloping terrain down to the pond. Visual impact is thus reduced to a minimum.

Okazaki Museum is the first in Japan to focus on the mind as its theme. The museum intends to hold temporary exhibitions on this subject while gradually increasing the number of works in the permanent collection.

introduced a more informal note. Modern museums include facilities which complement the exhibition galleries, making possible a wide range of activities in addition to those of a purely artistic nature.

Akira Kuryu has adapted the building perfectly to the sloping terrain, carefully graduating the visual impact of the building's volume. Visitors, after approaching through the "water axis," become aware of the transparent volume of the entrance hall. An alternate itinerary, however, also leads visitors by the pond across the terraces formed by the museum on the slope.

On the first level are the restaurant, library, and large entrance hall, conceived as an enormous skylight. On the intermediate level, the large central exhibition hall bordered by galleries forms the central body of the museum. On either side are areas intended for extra facilities such as seminar rooms, small projection rooms, and rest areas. The lower level, a few meters above the level of the pond, is almost entirely used as storage space.

The exterior image uses two distinct languages: that of transparency and that of opacity. On one side lies the large glass "box," an empty, transparent building that belongs to the poetic universe of the wind driving the windmills and of the steam rising from a central fountain. On the other side, almost hermetic blocks of concrete adapt to the sloping terrain. Passing between these two sides are the visitors.

The Okazaki Art and Historical Museum is a project that continues with this modern tradition that blends respect for its geographical and natural context with an interpretation of local historical and cultural values. It seeks to re-create the essence of space that draws directly on Japanese tradition, furnishing people with a place to find themselves.

At night, the museum changes. Certain elements disappear, others are transformed; pathways and the landscape are created by artificial lighting.

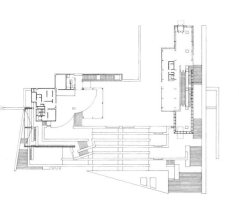

Upper floor.

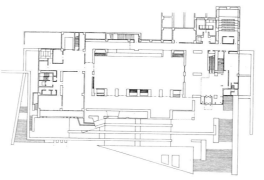

Middle floor.

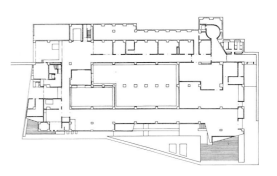

Lower floor.

Shoji Ueda Museum of Photography

Shin Takamatsu

The concept *Ma* defines both a spatial and a temporal interval. There is no difference between the two notions of time and space as understood in the western world. *Ma* is the pause, the silence between successive perceptions of the world and the self which continuously fade away and are reborn. *Ma* combines presence and absence in architecture, matter that dematerializes in the reflections of the polished glass, concrete surfaces, and water. Light that glows in the dark, nature manifesting itself in the geometry and structure of the works.

Traditional Japanese architecture is markedly horizontal and its spaces are not only non-geometric but also irregular. We might describe it as "formless" architecture, in which artificiality and nature come

together to create a kind of floating space. Western architectural spaces, in contrast, possess either a strong geometric factor, or a dynamic and predominantly vertical projection. Shin Takamatsu integrates these two opposing spatial ideas in the Shoji Ueda Museum of Photography. Located in bucolic surroundings and looking onto the Daisen volcano, this museum displays the work of the photographer Shoji Ueda, born in the Tottori district.

A site always possesses a special energy that affects people, and architecture can provide the answers and respond to the demands of a particular site. The logic of architecture must adapt to the hidden logic of nature in order for architecture and nature to coexist, albeit in conflict with one another. According to Takamatsu,

Location: *Kishimoto-cho, Tottori, Japan.*

Architect: *Shin Takamatsu & Associates.*

Design date: *1993.*

Completion date: *1995.*

Collaborators: *Yamamoto-Tachibana Architects & Engineers (construction), Architectural Environmental Laboratory (mechanical engineering).*

Photography: *Nacasa & Partners.*

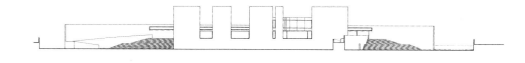

The irregular rhythm of the building, the sequence of solid and empty spaces, takes its inspiration from the relationship between photography and reality. As does the building itself, photography offers fixed images, torn from reality.

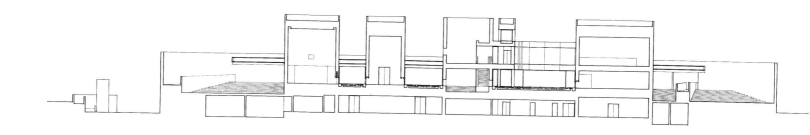

The museum is devoted to the work of
the Japanese photographer Shoji Ueda.

"There are two ways of relating architecture and nature: one is to search for harmony; the other is to frame the scenery within the architecture. This museum has adopted the latter." (Shin Takamatsu)

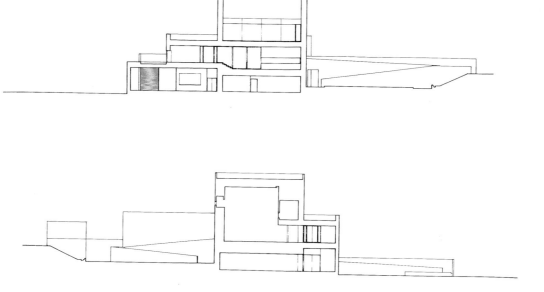

A circular wall guides the
visitors around the museum.

one must study the land to obtain a vision of architecture as being itself a place. Geometry is a symbol of human reasoning and transcends nature; it provides a global structure and at the same time contains fragments of various architectural scenes.

In the Shoji Ueda museum there is a sequence of four concrete volumes alternating with three spaces, all empty except for pools of water. The surface of the pools reflects the image of Mt. Daisen, a neighboring volcano, and its surroundings as if it were a photograph. Thus the landscape is captured and inserted into the architectural composition as if it were another museum piece. This effect suggests that through photography, we can also participate in new spatial experiences.

Concrete rises gently out of the ground. A large curved wall encloses the built-up space and faces it toward Mt. Daisen, an indication of its scale. Each volume contains an exhibition area, lighted through vertical and horizontal incisions; landscape paintings when seen from inside.

Time and the museum separate art from its context and enable us to appreciate it as an interplay of forms. Photography does the same with reality, presenting it as separate from its original surroundings.

The museum clearly faces Mt. Daisen in the background.

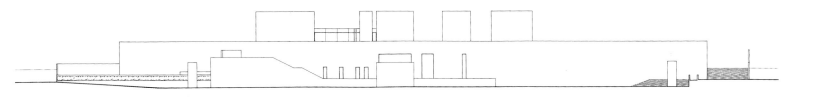

Two details of the patios between
the exhibition rooms, each
covered by a layer of water.

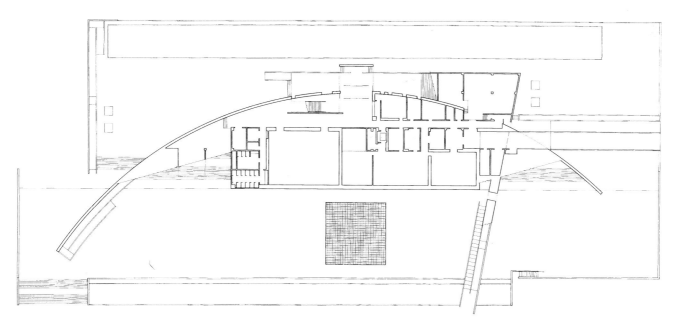

Ground floor.

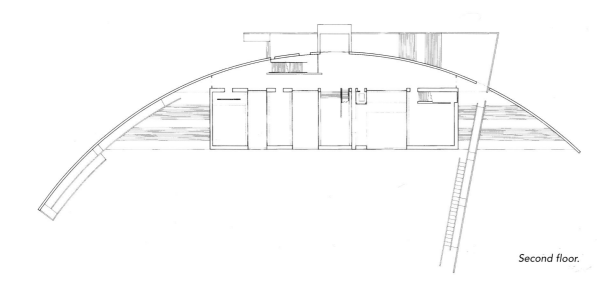

Second floor.

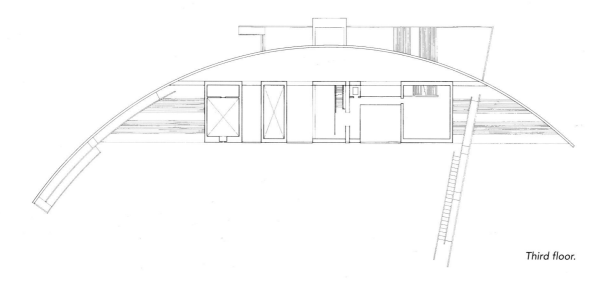

Third floor.

Detail of the staircase in the hall.

Detail of one of the rooms. Slides of photographs taken by Shoji Ueda are projected onto the white wall in the background. The windows are barely waist height, so that photographs can be hung over them at eye level.

Chikatsu-Asuka Historical Museum

Tadao Ando

The extraordinary coherence of Ando's works is based in a firm intellectual and theoretical foundation. Ando's architecture has a poetic and philosophical purpose. His buildings, with their pure geometric forms and simple materials, and their clear, open spaces, attempt to capture the variations of light throughout the day and throughout the seasons in a movement parallel to the itinerary followed by the visitors. In this way, Ando tries to confront man's subjective and linear perception of time against the continuous cycles reflected in a changing landscape.

It is obvious that for such an image to be effective, architecture must be reduced to essentials. This explains the lack of references and signs. The materials are almost always the same: concrete, unvarnished wood, glass, and steel. Forms are reduced to pure geometric volumes.

However, despite the undeniable coherence of all Ando's architecture, it is still possible to find conceptual differences, depending on the purpose for which the buildings are intended. Thus, Ando's single family units and churches have a character that is different from his museums, for example. Although Ando's houses, small temples, and sanctuaries possess a solemnity and mysticism rare in modern architecture, this

Location: *Minami-kawachi, Osaka.*
Design date: *1993.*
Completion date: *1994.*
Architect: *Tadao Ando.*
Photography: *Shigeo Ogawa.*

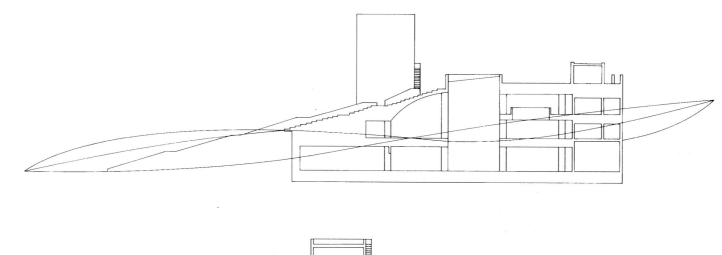

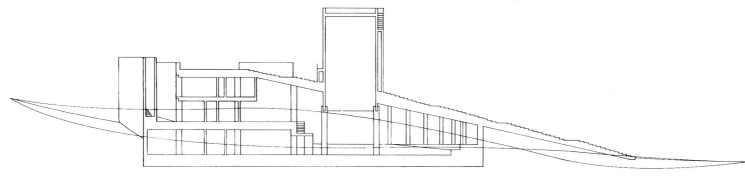

Sections.

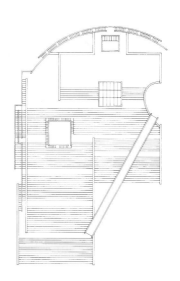

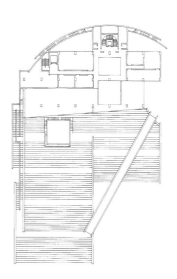

Roof plan.

Second floor.

First floor.

Basement.

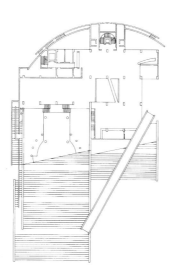

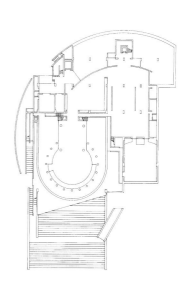

All Tadao Ando's architecture has a sequential nature. The Japanese architect has adopted Le Corbusier's idea of an architectural promenade. The project is based on an itinerary that unfolds as a series of moments, places, and experiences. In this museum, one reaches the interior only after walking along the paths surrounding the building and then ascending the monumental staircase. Entering the building thus becomes a ceremony.

View of the granite staircase, a concrete walkway leading directly to the entrance.

The exhibition rooms are relatively small in comparison to the building's monumental exterior.

The architect wishes to create the impression that the visitor is actually inside an ancient funerary temple.

mysticism evolves into monumentality in his large public works.

Over recent years Ando has built several museums: the Tombs Wood Museum in Kumamoto (1992), the Hyogo Wood Museum (1994), Osaka Suntory Museum (1994), Nariwa Municipal Museum (1997), apart from winning the competition for the Fort Worth Modern Art Museum over Louis Kahn's legendary Kimbell Museum. Yet perhaps the Chikatsu-Asuka Historical Museum is the best example of the monumental character of his architecture when approaching this kind of building.

This museum has an undeniable similarity with the great works of protohistorical cultures, such as the pyramids and the ziggurats. It is no coincidence that Chikatsu-Asuka, to the south of Osaka prefecture, was the social hub of the country during an earlier period of Japan's history. This area possesses one of the main collections of burial mounds (kofun) in Japan, with over two hundred tombs and cenotaphs, including four imperial tombs.

"The Chikatsu-Asuka Historical Museum is dedicated to exhibiting and researching kofun culture. In order to produce a museum integrated with the burial mounds, I have conceived it as a stepped hill, from which the visitor may have a panoramic view of the necropolis. Nearby, plum trees, a pond and paths among the surrounding hills envelop the museum in an environment conducive to outdoor activity. Its roof, which is really a large stepped plaza, will be used for drama and music festivals and other performances. Inside the building the display areas are dark and the objects are exhibited as they were found in the tombs. Visitors receive the sensation of entering an actual tomb and feel drawn, in mood, back to ancient times". (Tadao Ando)

General axonometric plan of the museum.

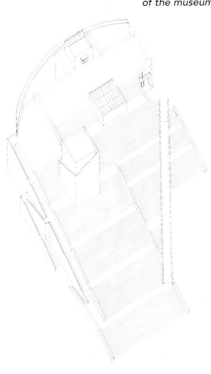

Museum of Modern Art and Wakayama Prefectural Museum

Kisho Kurokawa

Subsequent to the Modern Movement, Japanese architecture is noted principally for its open advocacy of the International Style and, at the same time, of a surprising formal intensity. This intensity and expressionism were enhanced in the 1950s by the integration of formal elements of traditional architecture; an abstract idea of domestic space, light roofs, wooden structures, and a special, constructivist sensitivity, all of which was heightened by the use of reinforced concrete. In other words, Japanese architects developed an affinity between modern architecture and traditional Japanese architecture. This aim is termed *wakonyosai* and consists of preserving the Japanese spirit while utilizing Western technology.

These new reinforced concrete and steel structures allow the construction of large, compact complexes that can accommodate a wide variety of activities, can be enlarged, and can also act on a much grander scale than a conventional building.

The search for a new type of architecture finds its means of expression in the proposals of the so-called Metabolist group, to which Kisho Kurokawa belongs. Their basic idea is to put forward proposals, ranging from industrial designs to urban

Location: *Wakayama, Japón.*
Client: *Wakayama Prefecture.*
Design date: *1991.*
Completion date: *1994.*
Collaborators: *Tasuaki Tanaka, Akira Yokohama, Hiroshi Kanematsu, Kazunori Uchida, Masahiro Kamei, Seiki Iwasaki, Nobuo Abe, Yukio Yoshida, Ichiro Tanaka, Naotake Ueki, Iwao Miura.*
Photography: *Tomio Ohashi.*

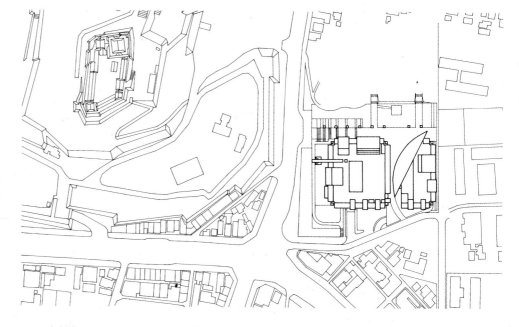

On the previous page, the entrance to the
Museum of Modern Art.

General view at night.

Axonometric plan of the museum complex.

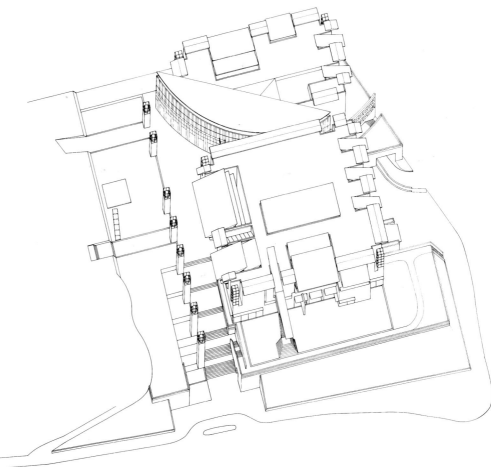

areas, in which technological developments and the systems of residential units are fundamental.

Metabolists aim to express the vision of a society in continuous evolution and to effect a transformation of vital and technological processes. Today, however, this stance has been somewhat modified. "Standardization was important in industrial society," explains Kurokawa, "but in the present information-led society, identity and distinction acquire more importance."

The museum is located in the gardens surrounding Wakayama castle which are now divided into two different areas. The architecture of castles was developed during the 16th and 17th centuries, the eaves

Staircase leading to the main entrance, adorned with eaves.

The eaves take their inspiration from traditional Japanese architecture. They are not a literal reproduction, however, but a reinterpretation which reveals the technical capacity of modern construction.

Detail of a lamp.

Night view of the skylights.

Cross section. The basement is shared by both museums.

being the most characteristic feature of this style. During the Second World War Wakayama castle was heavily bombed but it has now been renovated.

This direct contact with ancient buildings was the basis for transforming the formal and construction criteria of many architects. Such contact has opened a crisis in the Modern Movement with respect to pure forms and technology, restoring to a certain extent the aesthetic and tectonic sense of tradition.

The project comprises two buildings. The larger one contains the permanent and temporary international modern art exhibitions, and the smaller one accommodates exhibitions of local and regional interest. The architecture of this museum has incorporated traditional Japanese forms and reinterpreted them abstractly. It possesses the same curved eaves, yet uses modern materials and a more bold structural form. It also addresses the complex relationship between the interior and exterior, known in Japanese tradition under the name *engawa*, to create a kind of intermediate space.

Between the two buildings lies an empty space which in Eastern tradition does not possess negative connotations as it some-

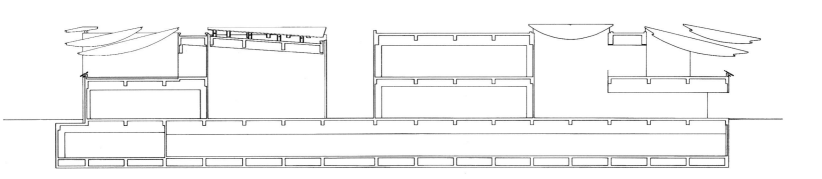

0 5 10

View of the main hall and one
of the exhibition rooms of the
Museum of Modern Art.

Basement.

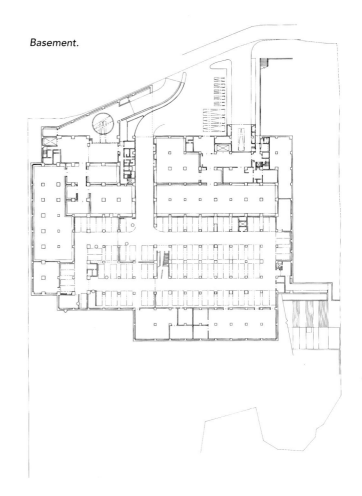

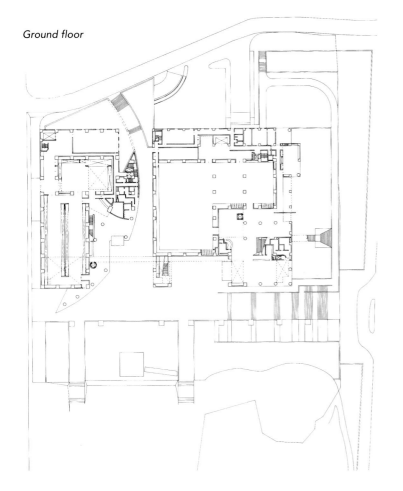

Ground floor

Second floor.

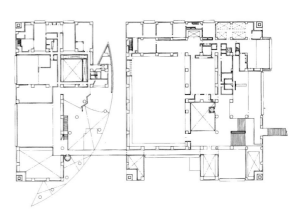

0   10   20

times does in the Western world. The void, in Japanese tradition, expresses the very essence of existence.

Both the art museum and the prefectural museum are designed using simple geometric forms. This simplicity and continuity of the ground floor space becomes more complex and asymmetric on reaching the façade, which is not a smooth, continuous line, but more of an irregular plane with insets and projecting points, lending it a greater expressive power.

There is an intermediate space between the exterior and interior, which can be accessed from an interior gallery.

On the following page, a detail of the library. The lamps are reminiscent of the lights outside and of traditional Japanese lamps.

Tadao Ando

1941. Born in Osaka, Japan.

1962-1969. Studies architecture on his own. Travels through the United States, Europe and Africa.

1969. Establishes Tadao Ando Architect & Associates.

1975. Azuma House.

1981. Koshino House, Hyogo.

1995. Pritzger Prize.

Major works between 1990-1997: Buddhist Water Temple, Hyogo; Japanese Pavilion at World Expo '92, Sevilla; Museum of the Forest of Tombs, Kumamoto; Rokko Housing Development; Vitra Conference Center, Weil am Rhein; Sanctuary Museum, Osaka; UNESCO Headquarters Meditation Area.

Mario Botta

1943. Born in Medrisio, Ticino, Switzerland.

1969. Graduates from the Institute of Architecture, Venice University.

1969. Begins working as an architect in Lugano.

Major works between 1990-1997: Church in Pordenone, Italy; Evry Cathedral, France; Swiss Bank in Basil, Switzerland; Church in Battista, Italy; Church in Satirana di Merate, Italy; Tinguely Museum, Basil.

William P. Bruder

1946. Born in Milwaukee, Wisconsin, USA.

1969. Graduates in Sculpture from University of Wisconsin.

1969-1974. Works for Gunner Birkerts Associate Architects.

1974. Establishes his own studio in Phoenix, Arizona.

Major works between 1990-1997:

Hill/Shepard House; Kol Ami Temple; Office building in Riddell, Wyoming; Central Library, Phoenix; Museum of Contemporary Art, Scottsdale.

Henri E. Ciriani

1936. Born in Lima, Peru.

1961. Graduates in Architecture and Urban Planning from the National University in Lima.

1961-1964. Works as an architect in Peru.

1964. Moves to France.

1965. Forms a partnership with Andre Gomis.

1982. Establishes his own firm in Paris.

Major works between 1990-1997: Museum in Peronne; School in Marne-la-Vallée; Museum of Archeology, Arles.

Frederick Fisher

1975. Graduates in Architecture and Urban Planning from UCLA.

1976-1978. Works with Frank O. Gehry Associates.

1978-1980. Co-founder of Fisher-Roberts. Company.

1980. Establishes Frederick Fisher & Partners

Major works between 1990-1997: Sean Kelly Gallery, New York; Bergamot Station Arts Complex, Los Angeles; Houston's Restaurant in Winter Park, Florida; Jerry Bruckheimer Films, Santa Monica; P.S. 1 Museum, New York.

Frank O. Gehry

1929. Born in Toronto, Canada.

1951. Graduates in Architecture from University of Southern California.

1953-1954. Works with Victor Gruen.

1957. Graduates in Urban Planning from Harvard University.

1957-1958. Works with Pereira & Lukman.

1962. Establishes Frank O. Gehry & Associates, Inc.

1978. Gehry House, Santa Monica.

1989. Pritzker Prize.

Major works between 1990-1997: Eurodisney Recreational Center, Paris; Vitra Headquarters, Basil; American Center, Paris; Frederick Weisman Museum, Minneapolis; Nationale-Nederlanden Offices, Prague; Guggenheim Museum, Bilbao.

Arata Isozaki

1931. Born in Oita, Japan.

1954. Graduates in Architecture from University of Tokyo.

1954-1963. Works for Kenzo Tange Studio.

1963. Establishes Arata Isozaki Atelier.

Major works between 1990-1997: Palau Sant Jordi, Barcelona; Disney Building, Florida; Kyoto Concert Hall; Twin Towers in Fukuoka; Japanese Center for Art and Technology in Cracow.

Rem Koolhaas

1944. Born in Rotterdam, Netherlands.

1972. Degree from Architectural Association of London.

1972. Study Grant for New York. Publishes "Delirious New York, a Retrospective Manifesto for Manhattan".

1975. Establishes the Office for Metropolitan Architecture (OMA) in Amsterdam along with Elia and Zoe Zenghelis and Madelon Vriesendorp.

Major works between 1990-1997: Lille Congress Center; Villa dell'Ava in Paris; Kunsthal Art Museum in Rotterdam.

Kisho Kurokawa

1934. Born in Nagoya, Japan.

1960. Graduates in Architecture from University of Tokyo.

1981. Co-founder of "Metabolism Movement"

1986. Honorary Fellow of Royal Institute of British Architects; Gold Medal from French Academy of Architecture.

1967. Japanese Grand Prize of Literature for his book Philosophy of Symbiosis.

1992. Japanese Art Academy Award for Nara City Museum of Photography, Japan.

Major works between 1990-1997: Lane Crawford Place Shopping Center, Singapore; Hotel Kyocera, Kagoshima; Melbourne Central; Fukui Art Museum; Kuala Lumpur International Airport, Malaysia.

Akira Kuryu

1973. Graduates from Wadesa University School of Architecture, Japan.

1973. Enters Maki & Associates.

1979. Professor, Tokyo University.

1979. Establishes Akira Kuryu & Associates.

Major works between 1990-1997: Uemura Naomi Memorial Museum; Tonami Tulip Gallery; Okazaki Museum of Art and History.

Søren Robert Lund

1962. Born in Copenhagen.

1989. Graduates from Copenhagen Royal Academy of Fine Arts.

1991. Establishes Soren Robert Lund, Architects Maa Par.

Major works between 1990-1997: Arken Museum of Modern Art; House in Allerod; The East Asiatic Company Museum.

Terry Pawson

1957. Born in Newcastle-upon-Tyne, United Kingdom.

1983. Graduates from Kingston Architecture School; finalist for Rome Award.

1984-1987. Works in Rome and then with Terry Farrell.

1987. Establishes Pawson Williams Architects in London.

Keith Williams

1958. Born in London, United Kingdom.

1983. Studies Architecture at Kingston and Greenwich Schools.

1984-1987. Works with Terry Farrell.

1987. Establishes Pawson Williams Architects in London.

Major works by Pawson-Williams between 1990-1997: Radio Studios for Heart FM; Urban planning, Cahors, France; Restoration of Birmingham Theater.

Renzo Piano

1937. Born in Genoa, Italy.

1964. Graduates from Milan School of Architecture.

1977. Centre Georges Pompidou.

Major works between 1990-1997: Residential Complex in Paris; Kansai Airport, Japan; Brancusi Museum, Paris.

Erik van Egeraat

1956. Born in Amsterdam.

1983. Co-founder of MECANOO Architects.

1984. Graduates from Technical University of Delft.

1995. Establishes EEA Erik van Egeraat Associated Architects.

Major works between 1990-1997 (with Mecanoo): Housing in Park Haagseweg, Amsterdam; ING Bank, Budapest; Almelo Public Library; Economics Department of Utrecht University.

Shin Takamatsu

1949. Born in Shimane Prefecture.

1971. Graduates in Architecture from University of Kyoto.

1980. Establishes Shin Takamatsu Architect & Associates.

Major works between 1990-1997: Trade Fair Center, Kunibiki, Shimane; Sakaiminato Symphony Hall, Tottori; Shiji Ueda Museum of Photography, Shimane.

Jean Michel Wilmotte

1948. Born in Soissons, France.

1975. Establishes Studio in Governor.

Major works between 1990-1997: Lyon Fine Arts Museum; Headquarters of Haut-Garonne Regional Government; Restoration of Louvre Richelieu Wing; Tokyo Hotel in Shibuya, Japan.